A PICTURE HISTORY OF CRIME

Bonnie and Cly

A PICTURE
HISTORY OF
CRIME

Edited by Sandy Lesberg

HADDINGTON
HOUSE

Distributed by The Bobbs-Merrill Co., Inc. Indianapolis • New York

A Haddington House Book

First Published 1976 by
Peebles Press International, Inc.
10 Columbus Circle, New York, New York 10019

Designed by Nicolai Canetti

Distributed by
The Bobbs-Merrill Co., Inc. in the U.S. and Canada

WHS Distributors in the U.K., Ireland, Australia, New Zealand
and South Africa

Meulenhoff-Bruna B.V. in the Netherlands

Printed and bound in the U.S.A.

2/79

JOHN WILKES BOOTH

John Wilkes Booth loved what he believed to be the antebellum South. He had acted there, been acclaimed by and moved among the most exquisite of the southern aristocracy. The South became Booth's adopted country, and he felt it was his sacred duty to destroy the tyrant who oppressed his homeland, Abraham Lincoln.

Booth had originally wanted to kidnap Lincoln in March of 1865 and force the Union to return Confederate prisoners or even sue for peace. The plot failed because Lincoln changed his plans, and the very next month Robert E. Lee surrendered to Grant at Appomattox and the war was over.

Liberation was transformed into revenge in Booth's mind, and kidnapping into murder. Booth and his fellow conspirators plotted to kill Lincoln, Vice-President Johnson and Secretary of State Seward. The man in charge of the Johnson assassination, George Atzerodt, backed out at the last minute. Seward's would-be assassin, Lewis Paine, managed to severely wound the Secretary but failed to kill him. Only Booth was successful, and that to a large extent because Lincoln's box at Ford's Theatre was unguarded.

On April 14, 1865 at a performance of the play "Our American Cousins," Booth slipped into the President's box and shot him in the head. Lincoln died the following morning. Booth escaped, injuring his leg in the process, and was fatally wounded some twelve days later. His co-conspirators, except for John H. Surratt who fled the country, were hanged.

John Wilkes Booth, posing in sartorial splendor for an acting role

BUTCH CASSIDY

By the time Butch Cassidy (Robert Parker) teamed up with the Sundance Kid (Harry Longbaugh), he had a long string of bank and train robberies behind him. Cassidy was a fair outlaw, never shooting when it wasn't necessary and always respecting bravery in his opponents. The story has it that Butch and his gang held up the Union Pacific's Overland Flyer outside of Wilcox, Wyoming in June, 1889. The express car guard refused to open the door to Cassidy, who promptly blew the whole side of the car off with dynamite, knocking the guard unconscious. Some of the gang wanted to kill the obstinate guard but Cassidy refused, saying anyone with that much courage deserved to live.

After successful or unsuccessful robberies, Butch and his gang would return to Hole-in-the-Wall, Colorado, a mountain hideout for outlaws. Here Cassidy and the Sundance Kid met in 1900. After pulling off a bank job and train robbery, the two left for South America with an adventure-hungry young school teacher, Etta Place. Settling in Argentina, they managed a number of bank holdups, with Etta scouting out the banks beforehand. Bolivian soldiers allegedly killed both Butch Cassidy and the Sundance Kid sometime in 1908 after they attempted a mine holdup, but many believe that only Longbaugh was killed and that Butch Cassidy returned to the United States to live out the rest of a long life in Johnny, Nevada.

TOP: **Butch Cassidy (Robert Parker)**
BOTTOM: **June 11, 1974 – Mrs. Lula Parker Betenson, 90, said her brother Butch Cassidy was not killed in South America with the Sundance Kid, but returned to the United States and lived for a good many years. At the opening of an Outlaw and Lawman Library in Logan, she said Butch was a good boy who got off on the wrong foot, "but he broke my mother's heart."**

BILLY THE KID

Billy the Kid

William "Billy the Kid" Bonney was fourteen when he killed his first man, and by the time he was dead at age twenty-one he had killed a man for every year of his life.

The Kid was born in New York, but raised in the West in Kansas, Colorado, and New Mexico. Bonney's stepfather was a miner in Silver City, New Mexico, and young Billy hung around with gunfighter Ed Moulton. Moulton had helped the boy out of a jam or two, and Billy managed to repay his debt by knifing a man to death who had been attacking his protector.

After that, Billy had to say good-bye to Silver City and spent the next few years roaming the Southwest, leaving a trail of dead Indians and poker players behind him. When he finally settled down again, it was on the ranch of an Englishman, John Tunstall, in southeastern New Mexico. Billy worshipped the refined Tunstall, and the gentleman in his turn looked upon the Kid with very fatherly feelings. It was Tunstall's murder in February, 1878 that set Billy the Kid on the war path again. He vowed to get Tunstall's murderers, and one by one they succumbed.

Billy apparently tired of running in 1879 and decided to turn state's evidence in a murder case in return for his freedom. New Mexico's Governor Wallace accepted the Kid's bargain but insisted the Kid stand trial, saying that this was only a formality and that he would be freed. Billy grew suspicious and fled. He was captured again in 1881 but managed to kill his jailers and escape a second time. Finally in July, 1881, in one of the most famous gun fights in the history of the West, Billy the Kid was shot in the dark by Sheriff Pat Garrett on the Maxwell Ranch near Fort Sumner, New Mexico.

THE JESSE JAMES GANG

Jesse James was an intelligent young man, a Southern loyalist, who eventually turned into a cold-blooded killer. At the age of seventeen, Jesse joined Quantrill's guerrillas in the Southern Cause and became one of the most notorious members of the group. With the end of the war, James's criminal career began and lasted for sixteen years until he was shot in the back by Bob Ford, one of his own gang.

His exploits were romanticized in dime novels and celebrated in the eastern press. He and his gang were given refuge all up and down the Kansas-Missouri border, and were revered by the Southern farmers as men who fought against Yankee domination. A small portion of the myth might have been true, but James and his cohorts were by now committed to a life outside the law. Their motives that might have initially been patriotic were thoroughly converted into financial gain. Jesse, his older brother Frank James, and their cousins, Cole, Bob, John and James Younger formed the nucleus of the gang. Together they robbed some fourteen banks and trains in the Missouri area. In 1875 they got away with $75,000 from the Missouri-Pacific express train near Otterville, Missouri. The gang broke up after the arrest of the Younger brothers in 1876, following an abortive attempt to rob the bank at Northfield, Minnesota of $45,000.

Without the Younger brothers, Frank and Jesse were forced to ride with less reputable criminals, like Charles and Robert Ford. In 1881, Missouri Governor Crittenden placed a $10,000 price on Jesse and Frank's heads. The Fords jumped at the chance, and on April 3, 1882 Bob Ford shot and killed Jesse while he had his back turned, straightening a picture on his living room wall. Ford thus became "that dirty little coward who shot Mr. Howard and layed poor Jesse in his grave," bringing an end to the career if not the legend of America's greatest criminal hero.

Jesse James – his name was a byword not only in America but throughout the world. In the thirty-five years he lived, his misdeeds filled page upon page of newspaper stories. John R. Musik (under the pen name of D.W. Stevens) wrote 209 novels exploiting the James Boys; his stories began in 1881 while Jesse was still alive. Frank Tousey made more money publishing these stories than the bandits did from all their holdups combined.

THE JESSE JAMES GANG

Cole Younger, Jesse's cousin, was born in Missouri in 1844. When the James gang was riding high, Cole and his brothers Bob and Jim joined that notorious outfit. In 1876 the Younger brothers were caught and sent to Minnesota State Penitentiary to serve life sentences. Bob Younger died in jail; Cole and James were paroled in 1901, and James committed suicide a year later. Though he spent a quarter of a century in jail, Cole was still a legendary figure and was able to make an honest living touring the country as a lecturer and later in one of the Wild West road shows. This photograph was taken just after Cole's release from prison. He died in 1916 at the age of 72.

Bob Ford, one of the later members of the James Gang, caught Jesse off guard and killed him for a dead-or-alive reward. He was later billed on vaudeville stages as the man who killed Jesse James.

Frank James lived out his life peacefully after being acquitted of his crimes and died on his farm near Excelsior Springs, Missouri in 1915.

BLACK JACK KETCHAM

"Black Jack" and his notorious outlaw gang terrorized the West with train robberies and murders. He was finally caught in Arizona and sentenced to be hung in the spring of 1899. The photograph shows him on the scaffold with the hood being adjusted by the sheriff.

CALAMITY JANE

"Calamity Jane"
(Martha Jane Burke,
nee Canary), the
famous frontier lady
sharpshooter of
the West

LUPO THE WOLF

Ignazio Saietta, nicknamed Lupo the Wolf, was the most important blackhander in the City of New York for thirty years. From 1890 to 1920, Saietta successfully terrorized the entire Harlem area. Unfortunately for Saietta, when he decided to branch out into counterfeiting, he was quickly apprehended by the Secret Service.

Blackhanding was really nothing more than extortion. Blackhanders like Saietta would simply threaten proposed victims with death unless they agreed to pay a certain amount. At the bottom of the extortion letter was often the outline of a hand which had been dipped in black ink, a psychological selling tool that proved highly successful.

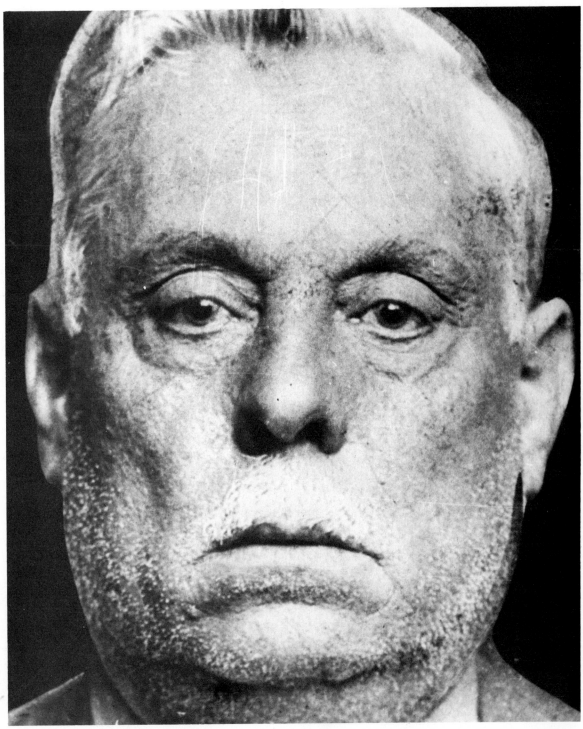

1936 – Ignazio Saietta, "Lupo the Wolf"

LIZZIE BORDEN

In 1892 Lizzie Borden was thirty-two years old and had a stepmother, Abby, who was only forty-two at the time. Lizzie and her sister, Emma, were extremely jealous of their mother's memory, and found it difficult to understand how their father could marry a woman twenty-seven years his junior.

On August 3, 1892 Mr. and Mrs. Borden were both taken ill with severe stomach pains. Strangely enough, Lizzie had bought some prussic acid just a day before. No connection was ever proved. The following day, Mr. and Mrs. Borden were found bludgeoned to death by an instrument that could have been an axe. They were actually murdered an hour apart.

The only person police felt could have committed the crime was Lizzie. She had given a confused story as to her whereabouts at the time of the murder and had even burned a dress the Sunday after the deaths.

Still, the evidence was not enough to prove conclusively that Lizzie had been the murderess, and she was set free. After her acquittal, Lizzie and her sister inherited an estate valued at close to half a million dollars. Lizzie remained in Fall River, Massachusetts until her natural death in 1927.

Lizzie Borden

HARRY K. THAW

"Dementia Americana" the psychiatrists called it, the belief that every man's wife was sacred. That's what they said Harry Kendall Thaw, the murderer of Stanford White, had. Around the turn of the century, socialite Harry Thaw married Floradora Girl Evelyn Nesbit, who had had a liaison with architect Stanford White. His wife's imagined relations with White were driving Thaw slowly mad, until on a European cruise he finally cracked up and beat his young wife into "confessing" her premarital sins.

Evelyn told all, even to the point of exaggeration. She detailed how White had tricked her into coming to his apartment in the tower of Madison Square Garden. He had plied her with drink to the point of oblivion. Upon awakening, she discovered herself *au naturel* and alone in bed with White.

Thaw became insane with jealousy. On the night of June 25, 1906 at the Madison Square Garden dining theatre, Evelyn pointed out White to her husband. Thaw rose, strolled over to White's table, and pumped three bullets into his head.

The jury found Thaw insane and sentenced him to be confined in the New York State Asylum at Matteawan, New York. He was released in 1915, only to be reincarcerated for whipping a teenage boy. He was released for a second time in 1922, and roamed the world spending his millions until his death in 1947.

Evelyn Nesbit

HARRY K. THAW

Stanford White

Harry Thaw and his mother

CHESTER GILLETTE

The American tragedy. A young man on the move. A hard worker determined to "make something out of himself." He falls in love with a society girl, with her social position and all its trappings. But he succumbs to sexual urges which can only be satisfied by the little shop girl, the girl who is sexually right, but socially wrong. Afterwards, he forgets the girl. She becomes pregnant and expects him to marry her. The young man sees his dreams go up in smoke, his future crumble. He puts her off, hopes she'll disappear, but she doesn't. He becomes desperate. He can't relinquish his dreams for what he considers an insipid reality. He takes the girl to a lake. She talks of marriage, he ignores her. He rents a boat and while on the deserted lake bludgeons her to death.

Theodore Dreiser wrote the book, but Chester Gillette and Grace "Billie" Brown unfortunately lived it in reality. On July 7, 1906 Gillette murdered Billie because her pregnancy was about to destroy his future. He denied the deed, but was convicted of murder and electrocuted on March 30, 1908.

TOP: **1906 – Chester Gillette**

BOTTOM: **1906 – Grace "Billie" Brown,
murder victim of Chester Gillette**

DR. HAWLEY CRIPPEN

Dr. and Mrs. Hawley Crippen were not the happiest of couples. He was a rather retiring gentleman, while she thirsted for a stage career. Mrs. Crippen had more stage names than she had roles, "Belle Elmore" being her favorite. Perhaps she loved stage names because her real one had been Kunigunde Mackamotzki. She was last seen alive on January 31, 1910. Dr. Crippen told their London friends she had been forced to return to America due to a relative's illness.

Soon after Belle's disappearance, Dr. Crippen was seen in public with a young woman, Ethel Le Neve, 27, who was wearing Mrs. Crippen's jewels. Hawley told inquiring friends that his wife had died of pneumonia in California, and shortly thereafter Ethel Le Neve moved into the Crippen home at 39 Hilldrop Crescent, North London.

Friends of Belle's became suspicious and informed the police. Chief Inspector Dew questioned Crippen and searched his house, but found nothing to indicate a crime had been committed. He was about to drop the case when Crippen and Le Neve vanished. The house was searched again, and a portion of Belle Elmore's body was discovered, whereupon a warrant was issued for the arrest of Crippen and Le Neve.

The two fugitives were on board the *SS Montrose* heading for Quebec, with Ethel disguised as Hawley's son. The ship's captain, who had read the circular on Crippen and Le Le Neve, became suspicious of Mr. Robinson and son when he saw the father being overly affectionate toward his rather effeminate offspring. The captain sent a wireless message (the first used in connection with a murder) to London, and Chief Inspector Dew was on his way to Quebec where he confronted Crippen and Le Neve.

Hawley Crippen was found guilty of murder in October, 1910 and was executed. Ethel was found not guilty of being an accessory. As a last request, "poor old Crippen", as many called him, asked to be buried with a photograph of his lovely young mistress.

Dr. Hawley Crippen, in disguise as Mr. Robinson

DR. HAWLEY CRIPPEN

Ethel Le Neve, as found on board ship dressed as a boy

Belle Elmore Crippen

DR. HAWLEY CRIPPEN

39 Hilldrop Crescent, near Tottenham Court Road, London. The Crippen home where the murder occurred

Dr. Crippen and Ethel Le Neve in the dock

CHARLES BECKER

Charles Becker was reputedly the most crooked cop who ever lived, and it's not difficult to see why. In 1911, Becker became the aide of New York City's new Police Commissioner, Rhinelander Waldo. At this time, New York was a rather wide open town as far as gambling, graft, and prostitution were concerned. Waldo decided it was time to do something about the Tenderloin area as well as Broadway, so he put Charles Becker in charge of Special Squad Number One. It was the Squad's job to crack down on all those elements besmirching the city.

What Becker did was to organize the graft, gambling, and prostitution under one gigantic hand, his own. He held the reins of New York's underworld so tight that it was estimated he made at least 25¢ on every criminal dollar. If people didn't pay up, Becker would have his strong arms like "Billiard Ball" (because he was as bald as one) Jack Rose do them financial or bodily harm. If anyone was courageous enough to defy Becker once, he rarely was twice.

Becker's undoing was a man named Herman "Beansie" Rosenthal, a gambler Becker had murdered. The new District Attorney, Whitman, was after Becker's hide. Through a witness Becker had forgotten to have killed, Whitman traced the getaway car in the Rosenthal murder to Billiard Ball Rose. Rose was hauled in and, when Becker failed to spring him as promised, he began to sing. Becker was indicted, tried, convicted and sentenced to death. He was electrocuted at Ossining on July 7, 1915.

Charles Becker

HENRI LANDRU, THE PARISIAN BLUEBEARD

Henri Desire Landru murdered eleven people – ten women and one boy. All of the women had wanted to become his wife, all became his victim. Landru operated primarily through advertisements in the newspaper, announcing himself a widower desirous of marriage, and the response was gratifying indeed.

In January, 1915 Landru murdered for the first time, taking the life of his fiancée, Madame Cuchet, and her son in their villa at Vernouille. As with his later victims, Landru assumed the lion's share of Mme. Cuchet's wealth. Landru murdered twice more at Vernouille, a Mme. Laborde-Line in June, 1915 and a Mme. Guillin in August, 1915.

Something must have soured Landru on Vernouille, for he moved to a villa at Gambais, a village south of Paris, in late 1915. It was here that he was to murder the remainder of his victims. The pattern was the same: first a meeting in Paris, love, a proposal to move to Gambais, purchase of a round-trip ticket for Landru and a one-way ticket for his mate, murder, disposal, enrichment.

In order of their disappearance: Mme. Guillin, 1915; Mme. Heon, December, 1915; Mme. Collomb, Christmas, 1916; Mlle. Andrée Babelay, April, 1917; Mme. Buisson, September, 1917; Mme. Jaume, November, 1917; Mme. Pascal, April, 1918; Mme. Marchadier, January, 1919. Unfortunately for Landru, two of the victims' families, Collomb and Buisson, were brought together by officials in Gambais. The families compared notes which eventually led to a search of Landru's villa at Gambais, Villa Ermitage, and his eventual arrest.

Throughout his trial Landru maintained his innocence and silence, even in the face of overwhelming evidence against him. The bodies of his victims were never found, except for some unidentified bones discovered in the furnace of the villa, but their clothing and papers were. Still, Landru maintained his composure and wit, at one point offering a woman who could not find a seat in the gallery his own in the dock. Landru was found guilty of murder and was guillotined on February 23, 1922.

Henri Landru

HENRI LANDRU

Victims of Henri Landru – Left to right. Top row: Mme. Cuchet, Mme. Laborde-Line, Mme. Guillin. Middle row: Mme. Heon, Mme. Collomb, Mlle. Babelay, Mme. Buisson. Bottom row: Mme. Jaume, Mme. Pascal, Mme. Marchadier

HENRI LANDRU

**Henri Landru's Villa
at Gambais**

HENRI LANDRU

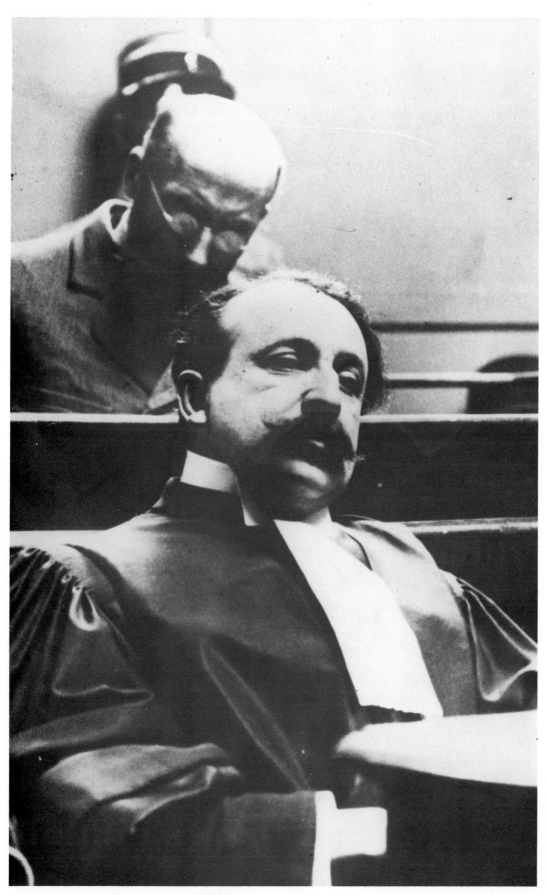

December 12, 1921 – Maitre Moro Giaffery, Landru's counsel, beginning his client's defense. Landru, background, is shown taking notes which he used in his address to the jury.

HENRI LANDRU

**1921 – Commissionaire
Danntel, who arrested
Landru**

HENRI LANDRU

**November 21, 1921 –
Henri Landru speak-
ing during his trial**

HENRI LANDRU

Henri Landru being led to the guillotine

CHARLES PONZI

In 1919, Charles Ponzi, until then a small time hustler, hit upon a scheme which would bring him in some $20,000,000 in eight months. Ponzi discovered that it was possible to purchase international postal union reply coupons at a depressed price in foreign countries such as France, and resell them in the United States for up to 50% profit.

When the word got out the people flocked to Ponzi, whose exchange offices were so unprepared for the financial onslaught that dollar bills had to be stuffed in closets, desk drawers, and even waste paper baskets for want of a better storage facility. When the newsmedia got suspicious and began to investigate, he slapped them with a half-million dollar lawsuit which quieted them down for a while.

Eventually though, the bubble burst and Ponzi was only capable of repaying 15 of the 20 million, which is amazing when one considers his extravagant life style (200 suits, 20 diamond stickpins, twenty-room mansion, etc.). Ponzi was jailed, released, jailed, released, and finally deported to Italy where Mussolini awaited the "financial wizard" with open arms. After a year or so the Italian treasury was lighter an undisclosed but sizable amount, and Ponzi had left for sunny Rio.

Charles Ponzi

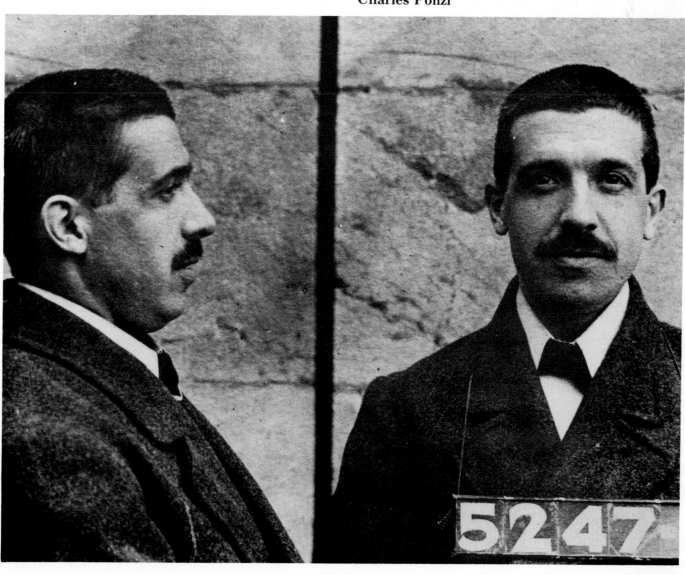

LEOPOLD AND LOEB

On the surface, it is difficult to imagine two more unlikely murderers than Nathan Leopold and Richard Loeb. Leopold was the son of multimillionaire shipping magnate Nathan F. Leopold and had been brought up in the prestigious Kenwood section of Chicago. He was graduated from the University of Chicago at age 18, and was an expert in languages, botany, and ornithology. Loeb was the son of a vice-president of Sears, Roebuck & Company. Also raised in Kenwood, he was graduated from the University of Chicago at the age of 17.

Both, however, had physical and, for their time, moral defects. Leopold had serious glandular problems and Loeb stuttered severely. Leopold engaged in perverse sexuality, fired by youthful encounters; Loeb was an overt homosexual.

Their criminal escapades began with Leopold's strong attraction to Loeb. Loeb agreed to homosexual encounters provided Leopold became his partner in crime as well. Leopold agreed and the two carried out a series of minor crimes before hitting upon the idea of committing the perfect murder. They looked upon the crime as fun, an intellectual exercise, a deed worthy of their superior intellects.

In May of 1924, after elaborate preparations, they kidnapped and murdered 14 year old Bobbie Franks and sent a ransom note to the boy's terrified mother. The child's body was discovered before the ransom was paid. Leopold and Loeb, confronted with their own amateurish mistakes – Leopold's eyeglasses at the burial site, copies of letters written by Leopold on the same typewriter as that used for the ransom note – admitted the crime.

They were defended by Clarence Darrow, who used the case to fight against capital punishment, and were sentenced to 99 years for murder and life for kidnapping. Twelve years later, in 1936, Loeb was stabbed to death while sexually molesting another inmate. Leopold died in 1971 while on parole in Puerto Rico.

Nathan Leopold and Richard Loeb

LEOPOLD AND LOEB

TOP: **CHICAGO, 1924 – Leopold (left) with Loeb (right) and their attorney, Clarence Darrow, during their arraignment for kidnapping and murder of Bobby Franks**

BOTTOM: **CHICAGO, July 22, 1924 – Leopold and Loeb before Judge Caverly, after Darrow entered the guilty plea**

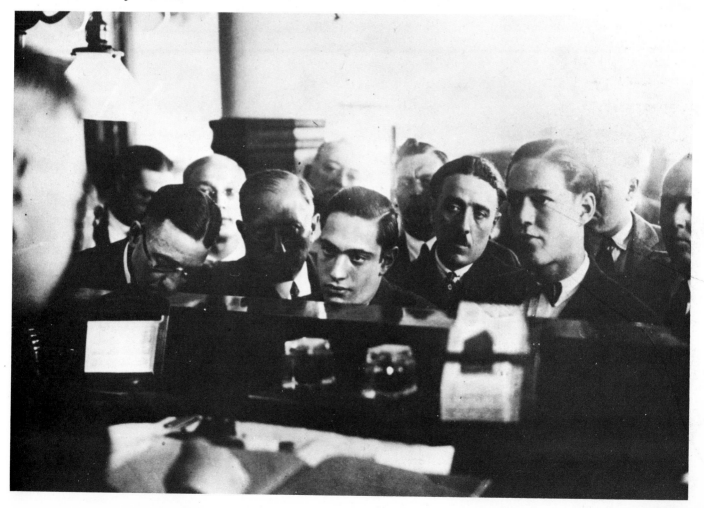

LEOPOLD AND LOEB

14-year-old Bobby Franks, the victim of murderers who set out to commit "the perfect crime"

LEOPOLD AND LOEB

**CHICAGO, 1924 – Leopold and Loeb, smiling
during their murder trial**

LEOPOLD AND LOEB

TOP: **CHICAGO, August 13, 1924** – Leopold and Loeb hold a conference with their brothers during a recess in the trial. The brothers all manifested a deep interest in each other and the conversations did not appear to lag for a moment. Left to right: Allen Loeb, Ernest Loeb, bailiff, Richard Loeb, another bailiff, Nathan Leopold, and Foreman Leopold

BOTTOM: **CHICAGO, 1924** – Nathan Leopold being examined by psychiatrists. Left to right: Dr. James Whitney Hall, Dr. William Hickson, Dr. Sanger Brown (standing), and Defense Attorney Ben C. Bachrach

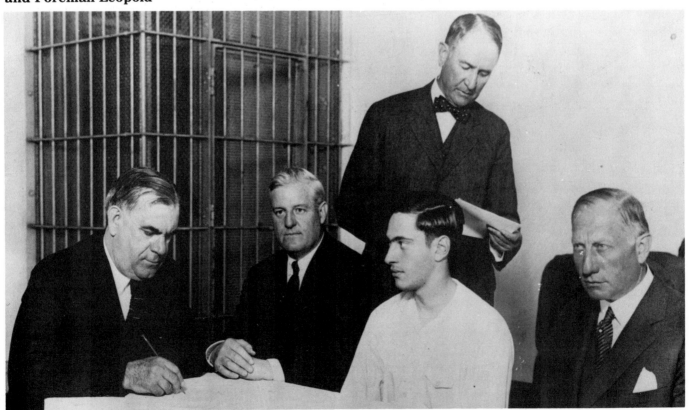

ALBERT FISH

Albert Fish was a sadist and a masochist. He enjoyed sticking needles into himself, hitting himself with a nail-studded paddle and having children beat him until he bled. Fish ate raw meat when the moon was full and read everything he could about cannibalism, carrying the best articles around with him.

Fish had grown up in an orphanage, which he always blamed for his aberrations. His wife had left him for a half-wit and, apparently no mental giant herself, had tried to move back in with her husband and children, with her lover in tow.

In 1928 Fish met a family named Budd and their lovely 12-year-old daughter, Grace. Using the alias Howard, Fish offered to take the girl to a party that she had wanted to attend. Instead, he took the girl to his cottage in Westchester County where he proceeded to strangle her. He then set about the business of cutting her up and making a stew out of the choicest parts.

The crime went unsolved until Fish wrote the Budd family a letter telling them their child was dead. The letter was traced back to him and after his arrest he readily admitted to five other murders. He also hinted that he had committed dozens of other murders and confessed to having molested somewhere in the neighborhood of four hundred children.

Fish was sentenced to death, but instead of a punishment, it was apparently the greatest thrill of his life. He even helped the executioner affix the electrodes. It took two massive jolts to kill the old man on January 16, 1936.

WHITE PLAINS, NEW YORK, March 12, 1935 – Albert Fish shown in a court anteroom as he looks at the outdoors through a barred and screened window during a recess of his trial

ALBERT FISH

WESTCHESTER COUNTY, NEW YORK, December 14, 1934 – Medical examiner Amos Squires directs policemen who are digging for bones at the spot where parts of the body of slain Grace Budd were found.

ALBERT FISH

WHITE PLAINS, NEW YORK, March 12, 1935 –
Albert Fish conferring with his attorney James
Dempsey during a court recess

ARNOLD ROTHSTEIN

Arnold Rothstein was a very important man, a genuine Mr. Big. He was called A.R. when only in his teens and as an adult never went out without his pocket money, some $200,000 in new $1,000 bills. His personal fortune, gleaned from gambling and prostitution, was estimated at $50 million.

In New York, there wasn't anything A.R. couldn't do. Want to sleep with a Broadway star, A.R. can put you there. Need something fixed with the law, A.R. can fix it. If he needed any muscle, there was always Jack "Legs" Diamond his chief enforcer. In 1919, it was Arnold Rothstein who turned the Chicago White Sox into the Black Sox by offering eight of them an estimated $70,000 to throw the first two games of the World Series.

For some unknown reason, Rothstein started to fall apart in 1928. He let himself go physically and, more important for a gambler, started losing tens of thousands of dollars. His bets just weren't paying off. Between the 8th and 10th of September, 1928, Mr. Big was involved in a mammoth poker game with two West Coast gamblers, "Nigger Nate" Raymond and "Titanic" Thompson. Rothstein managed to lose a total of $320,000 to the two of them. Worse, Mr. Big refused to pay, saying the game was rigged. A.R. was shot to death on November 4, 1928, and, not illogically, word had it that Thompson and Raymond were responsible, but they were never convicted.

1928 – Arnold Rothstein

ARNOLD ROTHSTEIN

"Nigger Nate" Raymond, who won $200,000 in a poker game with Rothstein

"Titanic" Thompson, West Coast gambler who, together with "Nigger Nate", was thought to be behind Rothstein's murder

JACK "LEGS" DIAMOND

There were many people who seriously believed that Jack "Legs" Diamond could not be killed. On at least three occasions he had been riddled with bullets and lived to tell about it. He had been wounded countless other times and popularly it was said that he jingled when he walked. "Legs" was mortal, however, as unknown gangsters proved on December 18, 1931 in Albany. But they had to kill him while he was asleep.

As with most of his compatriots, "Legs" Diamond had an impressive list of offenses, but nearly every charge was dismissed for lack of evidence. Diamond was primarily a racketeer and bootlegger who had been given his start in the garment industry by "Little Augie" Orgen. He later moved into narcotics. "Legs" Diamond lived to be 35 – a ripe old age by gangster standards.

THE CATSKILLS, NEW YORK – Jack "Legs" Diamond in court

JACK "LEGS" DIAMOND

THE CATSKILLS, NEW YORK, July 20, 1931 – In a raid on a retreat in New York's Catskill Mountains, police captured eight gunmen, who were believed to be waiting to kill "Legs" Diamond on his return to his Catskill stronghold. Their lair was fortified like a veritable arsenal with all types of arms. A dismantled, blood stained auto was also unearthed by police who believed that it had been used to take someone for a ride.

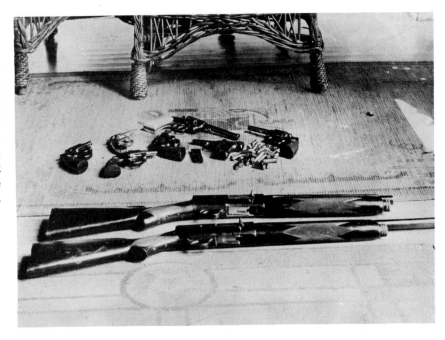

Charles Entratta, head of "Legs" Diamond's Goon Squad

JACK "LEGS" DIAMOND

1923 – Louis Cohen, charged with the shooting of Nathan "Kid Dropper" Kaplan on orders from Diamond

JACK "LEGS" DIAMOND

December 22, 1931 – "Legs" Diamond's funeral

BIG JIM COLOSIMO

James "Big Jim" Colosimo was a very classy pimp. He got his start as bag man for Mike Kenna and John Coughlin in Chicago. Soon, he met Victoria Moresco, a madam, who offered him the managership of her brothel. He accepted and they were married soon after.

Colosimo did very well with his ladies, owning some thirty-five $1 and $2 houses and two very posh establishments which catered to a high class clientele. Eventually, Colosimo branched out so that his enterprises included Colosimo's Cafe at 2126 South Wabash Avenue. Here one could meet Enrico Caruso, Dion O'Bannion, and Ring Lardner under Big Jim's gold and crystal chandeliers.

Unfortunately, Colosimo made a mistake. He brought his nephew Johnny Torrio west to deal with some blackhanders who were causing him trouble. Torrio did a good job, and Big Jim took him into the business. Johnny was a hard worker but he was also very ambitious, and when Colosimo rejected his suggestion in 1919 to enter the bootlegging business, Torrio sent for Al Capone.

Capone came west and started bagging for Torrio, but his real reason for being there was to hit Big Jim, and hit him he did on May 11, 1920. Colosimo was dead and Johnny Torrio was on top, at least for a while.

1920 – Big Jim Colosimo and his wife

JOHNNY TORRIO

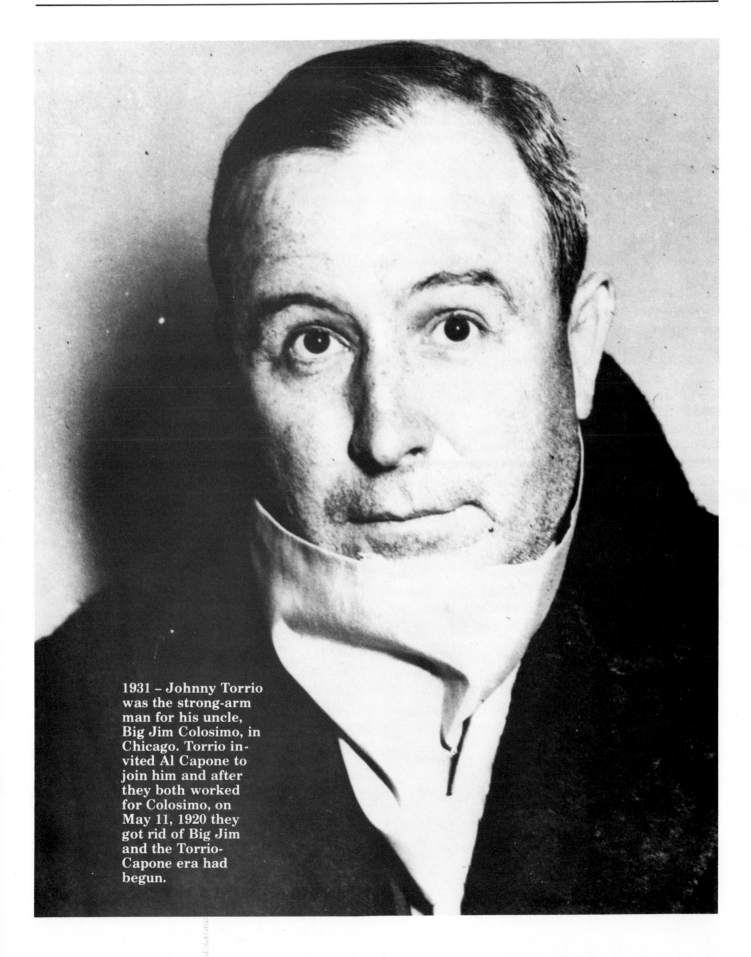

1931 – Johnny Torrio was the strong-arm man for his uncle, Big Jim Colosimo, in Chicago. Torrio invited Al Capone to join him and after they both worked for Colosimo, on May 11, 1920 they got rid of Big Jim and the Torrio-Capone era had begun.

AL CAPONE

Al "Scarface" Capone had started his career under Johnny Torrio's tutelage in Brooklyn's Five Points Gang. Scarface was a mover, and after he had laid Big Jim Colosimo to rest in Chicago, he was making eight to ten thousand a month as Torrio's aide. America's newest industry, bootlegging, was bringing in money by the bathtubful.

Torrio and Capone expanded their operations in Chicago as fast as they could, destroyng any sort of resistance as they met it. Most of Chicago's South Side posed little problem for them, but the North Side was different. The North Side was Dion O'Bannion's part of Chicago. O'Bannion had an organization almost as large as Torrio-Capone's and had a large number of police and judiciary on his payroll as well.

There was only one way in which the mastery of Chicago's underworld could be decided – total warfare. There had been minor skirmishes before, but on November 8, 1924 the war began in earnest. Three of Capone's men walked into O'Bannion's flower shop and murdered him. O'Bannion's friend, Earl "Hymie" Weiss, went berserk and vowed to kill Capone if it was the last thing he did. Hymie and "Bugs" Moran almost got Johnny Torrio, leaving him for dead on the sidewalk full of shotgun pellets, but Torrio survived his wounds and returned to Italy. Capone was now in full charge of the Gang.

In September, 1926 Weiss sent nine touring cars bristling with machine-gunners past Capone's Cicero hotel (his stronghold), firing 1,000 rounds at the building, hoping that at least one would catch Scarface. None did. Twenty-one days later, on October 11, Weiss was shot down and killed by Capone's gunmen while entering his headquarters.

A little over two years later, the final battle of the war was fought. Capone sent the last remaining member of O'Bannion's Gang a Valentine present in the form of five bogus police officers who raided "Bugs" Moran's bootleg headquarters on February 14, 1929. Six of Moran's mobsters and one non-gang member were lined up against the wall and shot.

It is estimated that over 1,000 people were killed in the war that left Capone Chicago's undisputed underworld king. It seemed as if he was invincible. He had amassed a fortune of over $50,000,000 and enough muscle to insure his position for a long time to come. The one thing Capone had not reckoned with though was public outrage over the bootleg wars and especially the St. Valentine's Day Massacre.

The heat was turned on in Washington and, although Capone could not be convicted for any of the murders he had ordered, the Federal Government did manage to convict him in 1931 of income tax evasion, sentencing him to eleven years. Capone was paroled in 1939 for good behavior and lived out the rest of his life on his estate at Palm Island, Florida. He was 48 years old when he died in January, 1947, some say of bronchial pneumonia, others of a brain hemorrhage; still others assert it was the last ravages of syphilis.

OPPOSITE PAGE: **CHICAGO, 1931 – Al "Scarface" Capone, on the eve of his trial and subsequent conviction for Federal income tax evasion**

AL CAPONE

Capone, on board a
train en route to
Federal prison

AL CAPONE

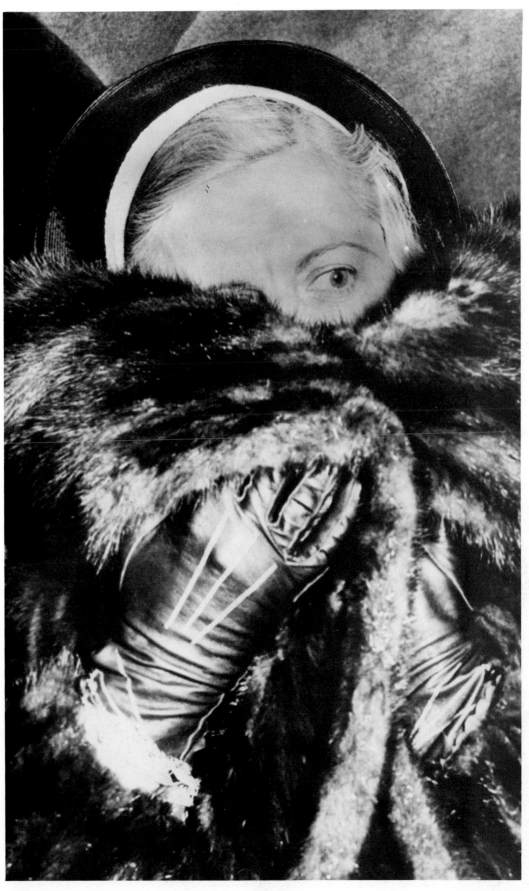

SAN FRANCISCO, December, 1937 – Seldom photographed, Al Capone's wife, Mae, is seen trying to avoid photographers in San Francisco after a visit to Alcatraz to see her husband. According to his last lawyer, John Kobler, Capone died penniless. Kobler also said that years later Mae rejected a publisher's offer of $50,000 for the story of her life with Capone, even though she was sorely in need of money at the time. "The public has one idea of my husband," she said. "I have another. I will treasure my memory and I will always love him."

AL CAPONE

**CHICAGO – Al Capone smiles as Chicago Cubs' Gabby Hartnett autographs
a baseball for Capone's 12-year-old son, Albert "Sonny" Capone.**

AL CAPONE

MIAMI, June 16, 1930 – Capone, on the left, being taken to jail following his arrest while watching a boxing bout in Miami. With Capone at the time of his arrest were his henchmen Nick Circella and Albert Prignano. This was the second time in a week that the police had arrested the harassed Chicago gang lord. He was booked for vagrancy under a new law passed, some say, just for the occasion.

AL CAPONE

1932 – Al Capone

FRANK NITTI

**1943 – Frank Nitti,
Al Capone's chief
enforcer**

FRANK NITTI

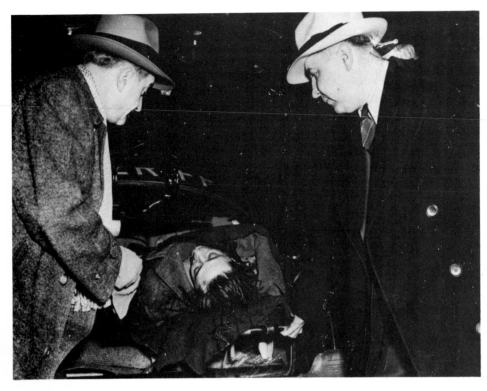

CHICAGO, March 19, 1943 – The body of Frank "The Enforcer" Nitti, being removed from the trunk of a police squad car. Nitti took his own life after a Federal grand jury had indicted him along with five others on charges of extorting more than $2 million from four large movie companies.

THE GENNA BROTHERS

The "Terrible Gennas" gather around the dining room table for a family portrait. Left to right: Sam, "Bloody Angelo", Peter, Tony, Jim, and families.

The Gennas were a tight Sicilian clan with a fearsome reputation in Chicago's "Little Italy."

Hit men for the Gennas were responsible for Dion O'Bannion's death. In the early 1920's, they coexisted with Capone by supplying bootleg liquor to his bars, but soon a deadly rivalry developed. Capone men eventually picked off the Genna brothers until their power dwindled.

DION O'BANNION

During the few short years during which Dion O'Bannion ruled Chicago's North Side, there was not a single bordello in the area – but that's just about the only thing that wasn't there. "Deanie", a regular churchgoer, was one of Chicago's most ruthless sons.

He began his professional criminal career as an enforcer for William Randolph Hearst's "Herald Examiner", making sure that newsstands took the Hearst paper instead of its rival.

O'Bannion soon became an independent with a penchant for safe cracking. He assembled a group of violent partners including Earl "Hymie" Weiss, Vincent "The Schemer" Drucci, and George "Bugs" Moran.

When prohibition came, O'Bannion had already bought some of Chicago's best breweries and distilleries, which gave him a big jump over the competition of Torrio-Capone. O'Bannion also took an active interest in Chicago politics, which amounted to stuffing ballot boxes as well as bribing election officials and candidates. He was also in his way a very big-hearted man, constantly paying hospital bills and sending presents to the people he shot by mistake.

According to many, "Deanie" O'Bannion was a lovable fellow. But not to Al Capone. Teaming up, Capone and the Gennas had O'Bannion murdered in his flower shop across from the Holy Name Cathedral on November 10, 1924.

1924 – Dion "Deanie" O'Bannion

DION O'BANNION

1926 – Earl "Hymie" Weiss was a boyhood friend, and later a hitman, of Dion O'Bannion. A ruthless murderer, "Hymie" invented the "one-way ride" used in gangland killings.

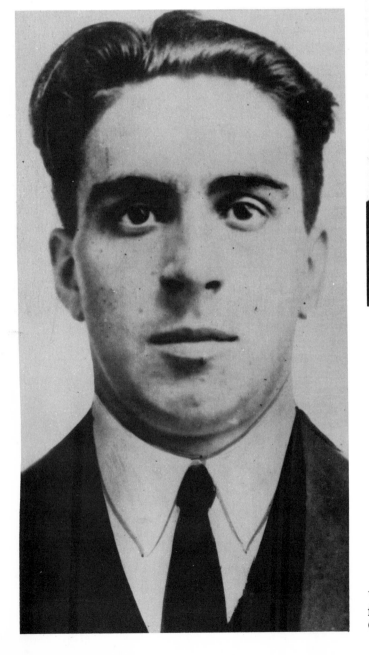

Vincent "The Schemer" Drucci, close friend and member of Dion O'Bannion's gang

DION O'BANNION

CHICAGO, 1924 – Flower shop owned by Dion O'Bannion, where he was shot and killed on November 10, 1924

GEORGE "BUGS" MORAN

George "Bugs" Moran was a part of Dion O'Bannion's gang on Chicago's North Side and was one of the main characters in the bootleg wars of the 1920's. It was Moran who, along with "Hymie" Weiss and Vincent Drucci, filled up ten touring cars with machine gun bearing mobsters and descended on Capone's fortress in Cicero, the Hawthorn Hotel.

The raid was enough to frighten anyone, but it wasn't enough to get Capone to leave the North Side alone. On February 14, 1929 Moran's gang was almost entirely wiped out in the St. Valentine's Day Massacre.

Moran was allowed one very small victory in that he and two friends were credited with the murder of "Machine Gun" Jack McGurn, one of the perpetrators of the massacre, some seven years later. But Moran was never again a force to be reckoned with in the Chicago underworld. He turned to petty crimes and small-time bank robberies, and died in prison in 1957.

DAYTON, OHIO, August 24, 1946 – Left to right: Virgil Summers, Mrs. Moran, George "Bugs" Moran, and Al Fonts in court being questioned in a $10,000 holdup of John Kurpe, Jr. in Dayton on June 28th.

"MACHINE GUN" JACK McGURN

James De Mora was an intelligent boy and a promising young boxer with the ring name Jack McGurn when his father was shot and killed in 1923. The Genna Brothers were held responsible and Jack decided to even the score by going to work for their rival Al Capone.

McGurn became an excellent "torpedo" for Capone, and earned his nickname through his choice of weapons. "Machine Gun" was ruthless and especially enjoyed killing a member of the Genna Brothers' gang for Capone. He machine-gunned six and placed a nickel in the palm of each dead man's hand to signify his contempt – nickel-and-dimers.

McGurn was allegedly one of the men responsible for the brutal St. Valentine's Day Massacre. The police picked him up for it, but the charges were dropped and McGurn was indicted for perjury. He responded by marrying the only person who could prove his guilt, Louise Rolfe, who, as his wife, could not testify against him.

After Capone was jailed for income tax evasion, McGurn slowly faded from the picture. Then in 1936, on the eve of St. Valentine's Day, an old score was settled and "Machine Gun" was shot to death. The police found a nickel in the palm of his right hand.

CHICAGO, 1931 – "Machine Gun" Jack McGurn with his bride Louise Rolfe

"MACHINE GUN" JACK McGURN

1929 – "Machine Gun" Jack McGurn

"MACHINE GUN" JACK McGURN

CHICAGO, February 14, 1936 – The body of "Machine Gun" Jack McGurn, local gangster, shown after he was killed in the Avenue Recreation Club. McGurn's death came exactly seven years after the notorious St. Valentine's Day Massacre, in which he was one of the chief suspects.

ST. VALENTINE'S DAY MASSACRE

Al Capone had fought first Dion O'Bannion, then Earl "Hymie" Weiss, and finally "Bugs" Moran in the so-called bootleg wars which raged in the streets of Chicago in the 1920's. O'Bannion had been killed in 1924, Weiss in 1926, and the last notable opponent to Capone's massive power was George "Bugs" Moran.

Capone had a compatriot, Abe Bernstein, who pretended to Moran that he had a load of hijacked booze available for Moran. "Bugs" had been dealing with Bernstein for some months and, unfortunately, had come to trust him. The delivery was to be made to Moran's North Side headquarters at 2122 North Clark Street on the morning of February 14, 1929. For some reason Moran was late for the delivery and as he arrived, he noticed three men dressed as policemen with two plainclothesmen entering 2122 North Clark. He dropped back and decided to wait. Minutes later, machine gun fire exploded leaving seven men dead and Moran's gang decimated.

Only one man was ever positively linked to the massacre, Fred R. "Killer" Burke, and he was never brought to trial for it. "Machine Gun" Jack McGurn was also supposed to have been a member of the firing squad, but he wasn't killed until seven years later on the eve of St. Valentine's Day, 1936.

OPPOSITE PAGE: **CHICAGO, February 14, 1929 – The St. Valentine's Day Massacre scene**

ST. VALENTINE'S DAY MASSACRE

CHICAGO, February 14, 1929 – The seven victims of the St. Valentine's Day Massacre ordered by Capone during Chicago's bootleg wars.

Left to right, top: Adam Heyer, Frank Foster, John May. Middle: Al Weinshank, Frank Clark, Frank Gusenberg. Bottom: Pete Gusenberg.

ST. VALENTINE'S DAY MASSACRE

ABOVE: **Fred Goetz (left) and Claude Haddox were named as participants in the Massacre.**

BELOW: **CHICAGO, February, 1929 – Garage at 2122 N. Clark Street, scene of St. Valentine's Day Massacre**

S·M·C·CARTAGE·CO
SHIPPING   PACKING
PHONE DIVERSEY 1471
LONG DISTANCE   HAULING

ST. VALENTINE'S DAY MASSACRE

CHICAGO, March 1, 1929 – "Machine Gun" Jack McGurn is questioned for the St. Valentine's Day Massacre. Left to right: States Attorney H.S. Ditchburne, John Stige, and McGurn

CHARLES BIRGER

BENTON, ILLINOIS, July 8, 1927 – Charles Birger (hat in hand), Southern Illinois gang chief on trial for murdering Mayor Adam of West City, Illinois

CHARLES BIRGER

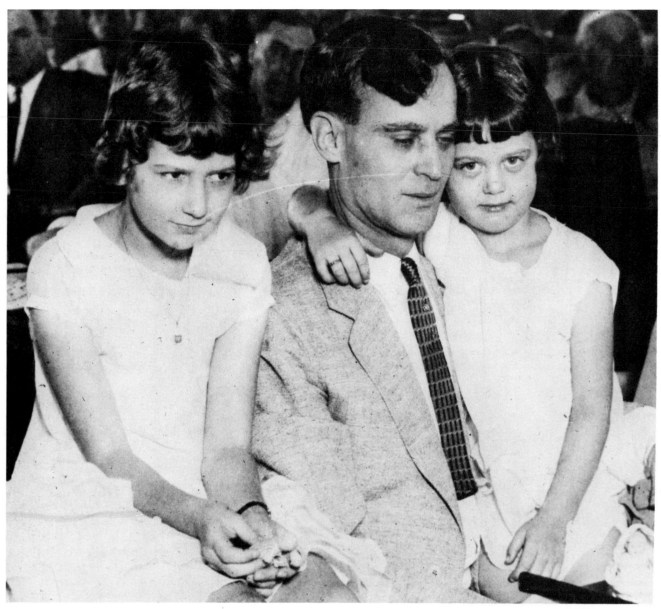

CHICAGO, April 19, 1928 – Gangster Charles Birger shown with daughters, Minnie (left) and Charlene, during the trial

CHARLES BIRGER

April 21, 1928 – This picture was taken just before the hood was slipped over Charles Birger's head. Phil Hanna, professional executioner, is standing behind him with the noose in his hand.

EDWARD "SPIKE" O'DONNELL

LOS ANGELES, April 20, 1934 – Leader of Chicago's South Side O'Donnells Gang, Edward "Spike" O'Donnell was an arch rival of Al Capone. The bootleg wars in the 1920's pitted Capone and various satellite Sicilian gangs against the Irish gangs who wanted control of the South Side. O'Donnell was arrested April 19 in the beginning of a drive by police to check up on eastern gangsters reported to have drifted out to Los Angeles early in 1934 in hopes of claiming undisputed territory.

ROGER TOUHY

Roger "The Terrible" Touhy was the gangless gangleader who managed to keep Al Capone at arm's length by simply bluffing. Touhy was an intelligent young man who had made enough honest money dabbling in oil leases to be able to start a trucking company in Des Plaines, Illinois in the early 1920's. The business did not blossom and Touhy decided to do what half the nation seemed to be doing, brew and sell bootleg beer. He was extremely successful because the beer was of high quality, the kegs (made in his own cooperage) didn't leak, and the cops and politicians were paid off in bottled beer brewed especially for them.

But Roger Touhy was doing too well. Al Capone got wind of his success and decided that Des Plaines was too much of a gold mine to let Touhy have it to himself. He sent a number of emissaries to Des Plaines, but they all came back terrified of the Touhy "Gang". But there was no gang. Every time the Capone men came down to visit, Touhy merely borrowed pistols and machine guns (some from the local police) and put on a show. He had locals tromp in and out muttering death to defiant and non-existent gangsters. He had the garage attendant call, and Touhy made vague threats over the phone, loud enough for Capone's men to hear.

Finally, however, Capone got the best of Touhy in 1933 by framing him in a kidnap case. Touhy was sentenced to 99 years for a kidnapping he had never committed. In 1959, the courts realized what had happened and released Touhy. Twenty-three days later, he lay dying on a Chicago street, the victim of an attack by unknown gunners.

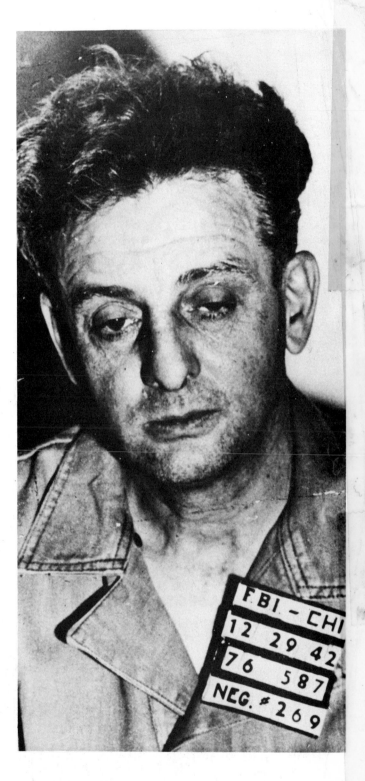

1942 – Roger Touhy

ROGER TOUHY

1957 – Roger Touhy speaking with reporters after his 99 year sentence was commuted to 77 years. He was ultimately released in 1959.

TOP: **CHICAGO, November 4, 1932** – These five men were among those taken by police during a raid in a richly appointed suite of offices. They were named by police as new leaders in Chicago crime.

Left to right: William "Klondike" O'Donnell, Labor and gang leader; William "Three Fingered Jack" White, killer and Labor czar; Murray Humphries, former Capone lieutenant, said to have entertained ambitions of succeeding Capone; Marcus "Steady" Looney, Labor racketeer; and Charles Fischetti, formerly Capone's chauffeur.

BOTTOM: **TRENTON, NEW JERSEY, June 13, 1930** – Several Capone men picked up and held for questioning in the killing of Jake Lingle. Left to right: Ed Morrison, Paul Ricca, and Augie Lavordo.

THE STAVISKY AFFAIR

Serge Alexander Stavisky was a swindler who precipitated a government crisis in France. A Ukrainian by birth, Stavisky had been involved in many private business swindles before graduating to public fraud in the early 1930's. For a time he actually was in control of the public finances of the city of Bayonne, France. His activities on behalf of the people of Bayonne netted him some two million pounds.

But the affair would have been impossible without the help of a large number of influential government officials, one of whom eventually became indiscrete. Stavisky's financial superstructure crumbled, and the financial genius shot himself.

That was not the end of the affair, as the political left and right promptly accused one another of complicity in Stavisky's dealings. One of the magistrates investigating the case, M. Prince, was found dead on the rail line near Dijon. Fascists accused socialists and vice versa. The inquiries ended leaving the public still ignorant of what had really happened but definitely poorer than it had been before.

PARIS, November 19, 1935 – Not the jury, but the Stavisky Case defendants – this dock at the Palais de Justice is crowded with its twenty defendants and the police officers who are guarding them. Owing to the prime political importance of the case, the courtroom was packed, and bedlam reigned until the seating was arranged. Mme. Arlette Stavisky, widow of the arch-swindler of France, is among the defendants, although she is not seen in this photograph.

THE STAVISKY AFFAIR

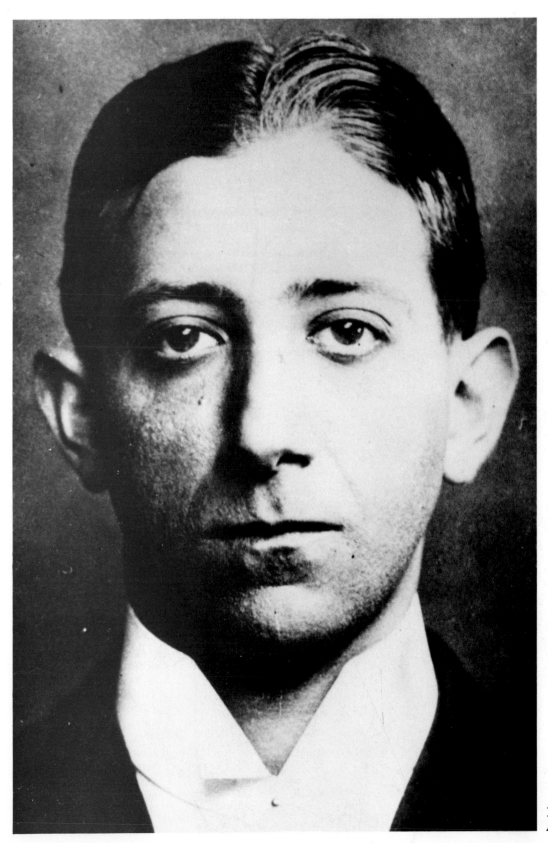

**1934 – Serge
Alexander Stavisky**

THE STAVISKY AFFAIR

PARIS, January 23, 1936 – Mme. Arletta Stavisky leaving the Palais de Justice following her acquittal. During the trial, many offers were received by Mme. Stavisky; offers of engagements on the stage, screen, and radio, and not a few offers of marriage. It is reported, however, that she turned a deaf ear to all of them except one that gave her an eight week engagement in a New York night club.

THE LINDBERGH KIDNAPPING

On March 1, 1932 Charles A. Lindbergh, Jr., the twenty-month-old son of Mr. and Mrs. Charles A. Lindbergh, was kidnapped and later found to have been murdered by a German immigrant carpenter, Bruno Richard Hauptmann.

Immediately, the case became of national importance as far as the child and publicity seekers were concerned. Even Al Capone tried to wangle his way out of jail in return for information concerning the kidnapping. (He had none.)

Approximately one month after the kidnapping, Lindbergh's go-between, Dr. John F. "Jafsie" Condon, made contact with a man known only as "Cemetery John", who had information about the child that only the kidnapper could have. He agreed to accept $50,000 as ransom for the child instead of the originally planned $70,000. The bills were all marked, including $20,000 in gold certificates. Cemetery John said that the child was on a boat at Martha's Vineyard, Massachusetts – he wasn't. The Lindberghs and the police had been duped.

One month later, a truck driver found a badly decomposed child's body, four miles away from the Lindbergh home, which was later identified as that of the Lindbergh child.

Some two years later, an alert gasoline station attendant noted the number of Bruno Hauptmann's car after the man had given him one of the gold certificates from the ransom payment. Hauptmann was arrested, stood trial, was convicted of kidnapping and murder and sentenced to death. He was electrocuted in the New Jersey State Prison on April 2, 1936.

FLEMINGTON, NEW JERSEY, January 8, 1935 – This is the original ransom note left by the kidnapper in the Lindbergh's nursery on the night of the kidnapping. It is signed with the peculiar symbol used by the kidnapper, distinctive in that it shows the $ sign after the ransom amount, i.e. 50,000$.

THE LINDBERGH KIDNAPPING

FLEMINGTON, NEW JERSEY, January 3, 1935 – Col. Charles Lindbergh leaving courtroom during a noon recess of the Hauptmann trial

THE LINDBERGH KIDNAPPING

FLEMINGTON, NEW JERSEY, February 9, 1935 – Mrs. Charles A. Lindbergh, mother of the slain baby, shown arriving at the courtroom to be a rebuttal witness in the trial of Bruno Hauptmann.

THE LINDBERGH KIDNAPPING

1935 – Bruno Hauptman, kidnapper and murderer of the Lindbergh baby

THE LINDBERGH KIDNAPPING

**FLEMINGTON, NEW JERSEY, January 10, 1935 – Hauptmann (center)
during his trial, seated between a New Jersey state trooper and
Deputy Sheriff Loeb Barry (right)**

THE LINDBERGH KIDNAPPING

FLEMINGTON, NEW
JERSEY, January
29, 1935 – Haupt-
mann in a meditative
pose before his con-
tinued questioning
on the stand

THE LINDBERGH KIDNAPPING

Dr. John F. "Jafsie" Condon, the go-between

THE LINDBERGH KIDNAPPING

FLEMINGTON, NEW JERSEY, February 16, 1935 – On the way to the
"last mile", Bruno Hauptmann is flanked by a state trooper and by Sheriff
Curtiss (right), as he is taken from the Hunterdon County jail at Flemington.
He is en route to the state prison at Trenton where Judge Trenchard
ruled that he must die in the electric chair the week of March 18th.
At Trenton, he was placed in the death house under heavy guard. This is
his first picture in handcuffs.

THE KANSAS CITY MASSACRE

Frank "Jelly" Nash, bankrobber, had escaped from Leavenworth in 1930 and taken up with the Barker-Karpis Gang. When the pressure was on the gang, he left and sought refuge in Hot Springs, Arkansas. There he was cornered by the FBI in 1933. Nash was escorted by FBI and police officials to Kansas City where a very special welcome awaited him.

As the officers and Nash climbed into a waiting car at Union Station on June 17, 1933, a large man carrying a machine gun told them to "get 'em up". All but one officer did, and then came a rain of bullets. The car was sprayed from front to back with the end result being five dead: one FBI official, three police officials and "Jelly" Nash. Supposedly, the men had been trying to "free" Nash, but the way in which the attempt took place makes it look more like a "hit" than an escape attempt.

Witnesses said they thought the machine gunner was Charles "Pretty Boy" Floyd, but Floyd vehemently denied having had anything to do with the massacre. Years later a ganster named Blackie Audett supported Floyd's claim by naming Maurice Denning, Verne Miller, and William "Solly" Weissman as the real killers. The gunmen were never captured and some crime historians believe they too were murdered because they knew who had wanted Frank Nash killed.

1933 – Frank "Jelly" Nash

THE KANSAS CITY MASSACRE

KANSAS CITY, MISSOURI, June 17, 1933 – Aftermath of the Kansas City Massacre shows the bullet-sprayed cars and two of the four police officers killed in a gun battle outside the railroad depot. Frank Nash, the convict they were escorting, was also killed.

JOSEPH ZANGARA

In February, 1933 Joseph Zangara, like countless other Americans, was unemployed. He had been a mill hand in New Jersey and when laid off had traveled south to Florida in search of both warmth and employment. A pseudo-Marxist, Zangara had become more and more crazed by what he felt were systemic causes of his unemployment, of which Franklin Roosevelt was the chief symbol.

Zangara learned from the newspaper that President Roosevelt was making a trip to Miami with Chicago Mayor Anton Cermak and made preparations to shoot the President. Roosevelt and Cermak drove through Miami in an open car and the cheering crowds broke through police barriers, bringing the speed of the President's car to a crawl.

Zangara had been waiting for Roosevelt to pass and when he saw the slow progress the car was making, he waded into the crowd, pushing toward the vehicle. Finally, with a clear shot at Roosevelt, he shouted, "Too many people are starving to death," and fired wildly at the President. The pistol was knocked from his hand, but not before Zangara had managed to kill Mayor Cermak. Roosevelt was unharmed. Zangara was sentenced to death and executed.

MIAMI, February, 1933 – Joseph Zangara, in the custody of Sheriff Dan Hardie (left), after his attempted assassination of President Franklin D. Roosevelt. L. G. Crews (right) holds the pistol which Zangara used.

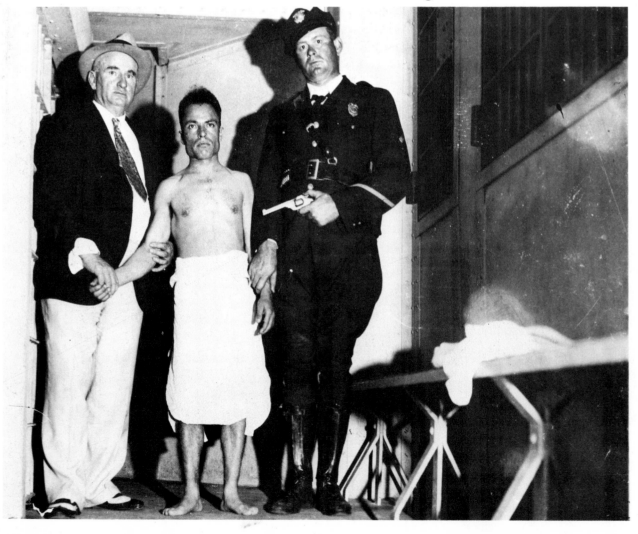

GEORGE "MACHINE GUN" KELLY

George Kelly married Kathryn Shannon in 1927 and from that point on his life was hell. Kathryn had been brought up in the backwoods of Mississippi and she had dreamt of riches and power. Kelly was a good-natured slob, a bootlegger who spilled more than he delivered.

When Kelly and Kathryn met, one of the first things she did was buy him a shiny, new machine gun. She made him practice as well, shooting walnuts off a fence. George liked booze more than he did machine guns, and had trouble landing a job. Finally, Kathryn found him one with a two-bit gang, and George helped rob the bank at Tupelo,

Mississippi, followed by the bank in Wilmer, Texas. Both jobs were small to say the least.

Kathryn was dissatisfied and in 1933 talked George into kidnapping oil millionaire Charles Urschel. The kidnapping was somehow successful, and after a number of false starts the gang collected $200,000 for Urschel's safe release. Soon afterwards, the whole gang was captured. George and Kathryn went to prison where he died in 1954. Kathryn was released in 1958.

October, 1933 – George "Machine Gun" Kelly (shirtsleeves) in Federal Court on trial for the Urschel kidnapping case

GEORGE "MACHINE GUN" KELLY

Mrs. Kathryn Kelly

BONNIE AND CLYDE

For all the folklore that has surrounded them, Bonnie Parker and Clyde Barrow were basically a couple of small time hoodlums – thrill seekers during the bleak Depression years in the Southwest dustbowl. They met in 1930 while Bonnie's husband was serving a 99 year sentence for murder and teamed up in 1932. W. D. Jones, an 18-year-old gas station attendant, joined the two outlaws for a time later that year. Clyde's brother Buck and his wife Blanche also joined up for a few months until both were wounded and captured in July, 1933.

The largest take the Barrow Gang ever had was $1,500, and they contented themselves mostly with gas stations, grocery stores, and an occasional small town bank. They were people who murdered just for fun or because someone said something they didn't like. Among them, they killed thirteen people.

Their escapades seem, in retrospect, almost suicidal. Clyde had sworn in 1932 that he would never go back to prison, while Bonnie, some few months before her death, made her mother promise to bring her home after they shot her.

They died, as hard and fiercely as they had lived, in May of 1934 when they were ambushed by a posse in Louisianna and killed in a rain of 187 bullets; Clyde was 25 and Bonnie was 23.

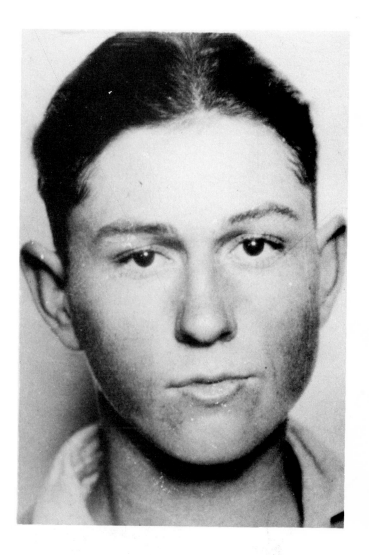

Young Clyde Barrow

BONNIE AND CLYDE

**1933 – Bonnie Parker
and Clyde Barrow**

BONNIE AND CLYDE

1933 – Clyde Barrow

BONNIE AND CLYDE

JOPLIN, MISSOURI, 1933 – This picture was reproduced from one of six negatives found in a gunmen's rendezvous after two men and two women had shot their way out of a police trap. An unfinished poem entitled "Suicide Sal" was found near the films, bearing the signature Bonnie Parker. Joplin police distributed this photograph as "Suicide Sal" and "Bonnie Parker".

BONNIE AND CLYDE

1933 – Clyde Barrow displays his arsenal.

TOP: **May, 1934 – The posse led by Texas Ranger Frank Hamer who slew Bonnie Parker and Clyde Barrow. Left to right, top row: Ted Hurton, P. Moakley, B. M. Gault. Bottom row: Bob Aleorn, Henderson Jordon and Frank Hamer.**

BOTTOM: **May, 1934 – The bullet-riddled car in which Bonnie and Clyde were killed in ambush near Giland, Louisianna**

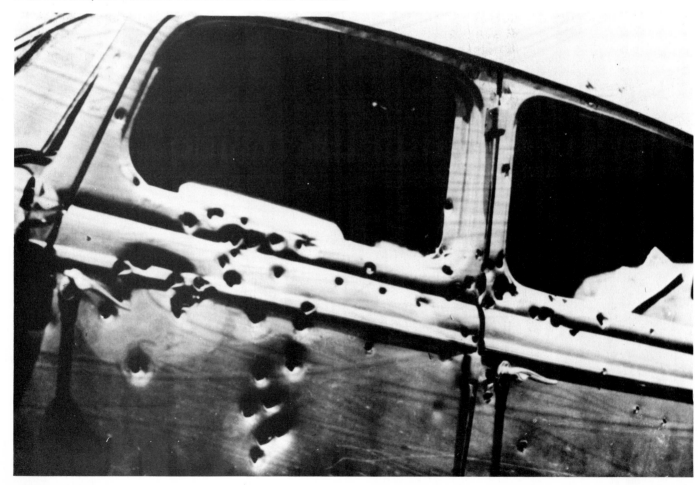

JOHN DILLINGER

John Herbert Dillinger was the consumate bank robber. Together with members of his various gangs, he managed to rob over ten banks, but it is not so much the number which is impressive as the manner and style with which Dillinger carried out his raids on America's financial institutions. His bank robberies were always meticulously planned, with gang members studying the bank beforehand, diagrams being drawn, and the time being clocked in which the gang could safely complete its operations.

During the robbery itself, Dillinger would often spring over the railing which led to the tellers' cages, an action which could almost be designated his calling card. Dillinger was also a very cautious person when it came to human life, and it was very seldom that people were injured or killed during his robberies.

Dillinger was not only a bank robber, but something of an escape artist as well. He helped ten convicts, including his pals Harry Pierpont and John Hamilton, escape from the Michigan City, Indiana State Prison; he was freed by Pierpont and company from the Lima, Ohio jail; he managed to escape from the Crown Point, Indiana jail by brandishing a whittled wooden pistol, while the jail was being specially guarded to prevent breakouts. Dillinger also managed to escape a large number of police and FBI traps. Part of his success was sheer luck, but part was no doubt due to his cunning and innate ability to react quickly to a dangerous situation.

But perhaps the greatest escape of all was Dillinger's last. The FBI, still smarting from an abortive attempt to capture the bank robber, had been made an offer by a crooked policeman and a prostitute to deliver Dillinger, provided the FBI shot him on the spot. The bureau accepted the offer and staked out the Biograph Theatre in Chicago. On the night of July 2, 1934, the young prostitute, Anna Sage, led "Dillinger" into the FBI trap, where he was shot and killed.

The autopsy report was lost for over thirty years, and when it turned up there were seemingly glaring discrepancies between it and the man people had accepted as John Dillinger. For instance, the murdered man's eyes were brown, Dillinger's were blue. Many feel that John Dillinger had made his last great escape. At any rate, he was never heard from again.

JOHN DILLINGER

**John Dillinger
at age 10**

JOHN DILLINGER

John Dillinger

JOHN DILLINGER

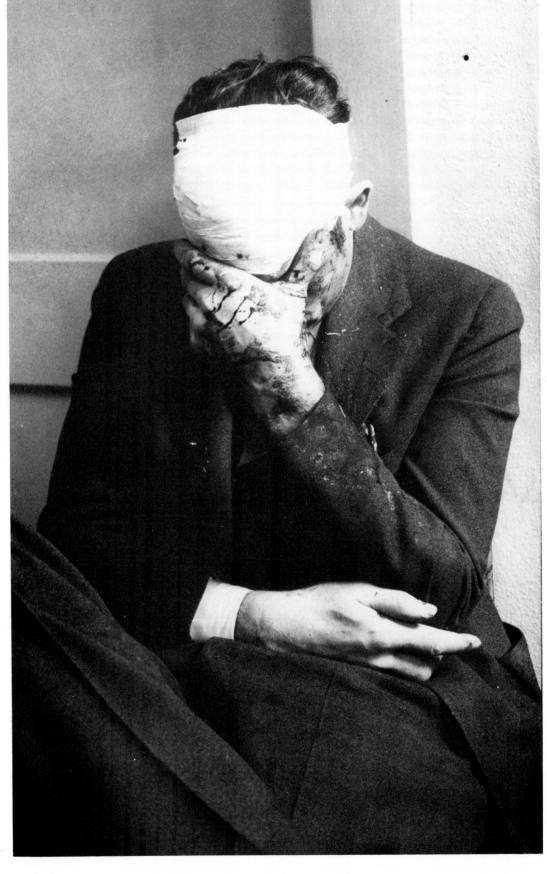

ARIZONA, January 27, 1934 – Russell Clark shown in his cell after his capture with three other members of the John Dillinger band of Indiana outlaws. Acting on the tip of a detective story fan, Tucson police rounded up the four men and four women, some claiming to be the wives of the men. In custody along with Clark were John Dillinger, Charles Makley and Harry Pierpont.

JOHN DILLINGER

MEMPHIS, TENNESSEE, January 31, 1934 – John Dillinger, securely shackled
to police officers, is shown here as he changed planes in Memphis en route
to East Chicago, Indiana, where he will be tried on charges of killing a
policeman. Left to right: Carroll Holley, Sheriff of Lake County, Indiana;
Dillinger; and Hobard Wilgus, police officer of East Chicago.

JOHN DILLINGER

  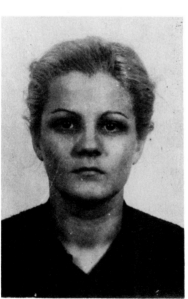

CHICAGO, September 1, 1934 – Shown are six of the seven alleged confederates of the late John Dillinger, taken in custody here. Left to right, top row: Arthur W. O'Leary; Dr. Harold Bernard; and Dr. Wilhelm Loeser. Bottom row: Ella and William Finerty, and Marie Conforti, said to be a sweetheart of the late Homer Van Meter, the bank robber who became Dillinger's right-hand man until he was gunned down in August, 1934.

JOHN DILLINGER

Harry Pierpont, close friend and member of Dillinger's gang

JOHN DILLINGER

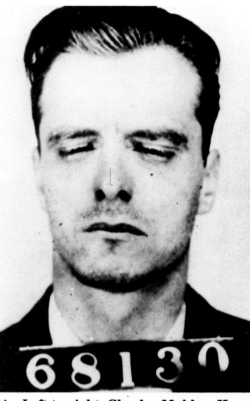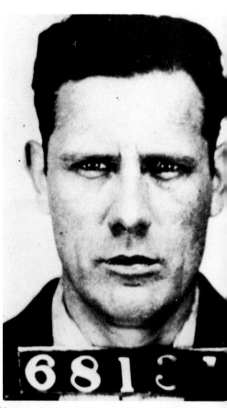

COLUMBUS, OHIO, April 21, 1934 – Left to right: Charles Makley, Harry Pierpont, and Russell Clark, to be known henceforth by their numbers as new convicts in the Ohio State Penitentiary. The three were convicted of killing Sheriff Jesse Sarber at Lima, while liberating John Dillinger from jail. Makley and Pierpont are scheduled to be executed July 13th. Clark is serving a life sentence.

JOHN DILLINGER

Mrs. Anna Miller Sage, the "Lady in Red" who helped set up Dillinger

JOHN DILLINGER

CHICAGO, July 22, 1934 – Federal agents caught up with the man they believed to be John Dillinger and killed him as he was leaving the Biograph Theatre with Anna Sage. This photo shows the front of the small theatre after the shooting. The picture he was seeing was "Manhattan Melodrama", a picture about criminals.

JOHN DILLINGER

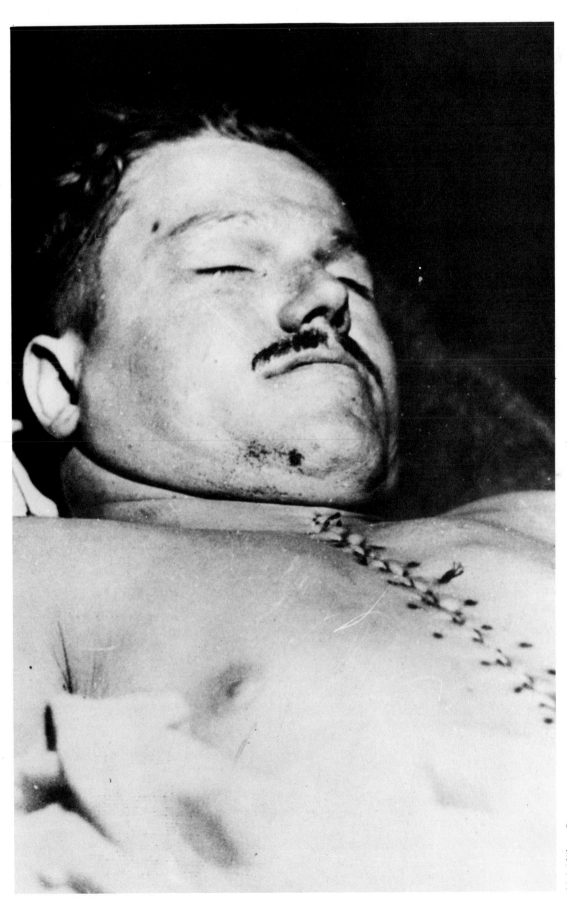

CHICAGO, July 22, 1934 – The man believed to be John Dillinger, in the morgue

JOHN DILLINGER

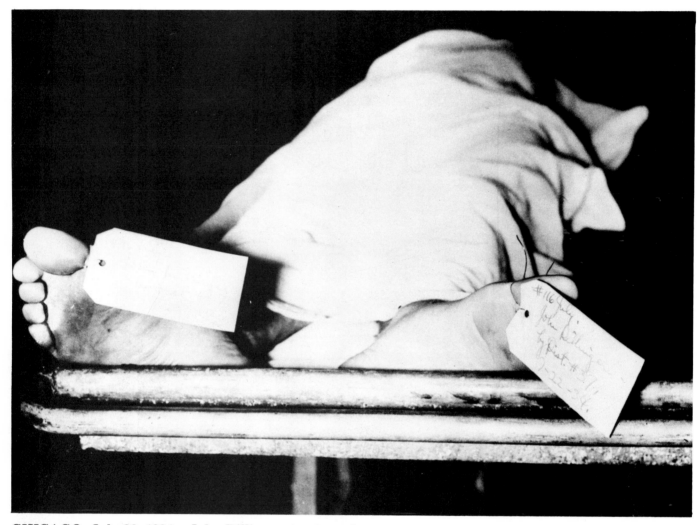

CHICAGO, July 22, 1934 – John Dillinger, toe tagged

"PRETTY BOY" FLOYD

Charles "Pretty Boy" Floyd was a strong man and a hard worker who, unable to earn a living in an accepted manner, turned to robbing banks. Whether or not he was a folk hero worthy of the name is a difficult question. Floyd murdered a number of men and was even accused of being the machine gunner in the Kansas City Massacre, something he denied.

It has been reported that Floyd tore up first mortgages when he robbed banks, in the hope that the mortgages had not been recorded. Floyd was an Okie, and he was understood by the Okies. They all knew what it was like to want to earn a good living and have a home, and to be frustrated at every turn during the hard depression days. Right or wrong, the banks became their special enemies. "Pretty Boy" Floyd was shot to death by FBI men near East Liverpool, Ohio on October 22, 1934.

Charles "Pretty Boy" Floyd

"PRETTY BOY" FLOYD

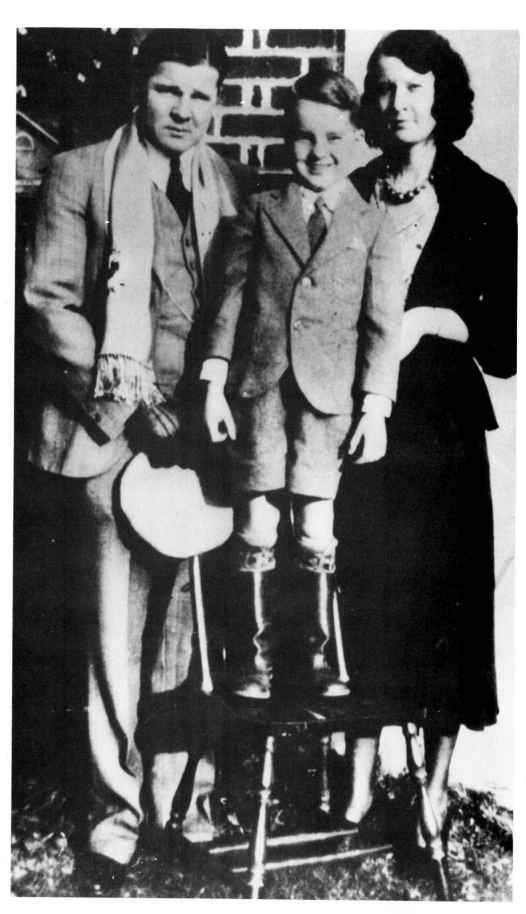

1934 – This is the last photo made of "Pretty Boy" Floyd before his death. With him are his wife and nine-year-old son, Charles Dempsey Floyd.

THE BARKER GANG

There were three reasons why it was very difficult for law enforcement officials to pin crimes on and apprehend the Barker Gang: the gang constantly changed its area of operation, it was always changing its mode of operation, and it made an awful lot of money. The Barkers could slip into a "safe" town such as St. Paul, Minnesota, where police and city officials could be counted on to keep quiet for a goodly amount of cash.

"Ma" Barker, her sons Arthur "Doc" and Freddie, and Alvin Karpis were the pillars of the Barker Gang, with "Ma" doing the thinking and the boys the execution. The system worked as the Barker Gang robbed banks of $250,000, $20,000, $150,000 and $47,000. They also got $100,000 and $200,000 respectively for the Hamm and Bremer kidnappings.

Unfortunately, a fingerprint was left behind at the scene of the second kidnapping and the heat was on. Freddie and Alvin Karpis tried to change their looks and fingerprints through plastic surgery, but only succeeded in causing themselves a great deal of pain.

Karpis left the gang. "Doc" was picked up in Chicago and died attempting to escape from Alcatraz in 1939. "Ma" and Freddie were killed in a 45-minute shoot out with the FBI in their Florida hideout. Herman Barker had committed suicide in 1927. The last brother, Lloyd, was released from prison in 1947 after serving a twenty-five-year sentence for armed robbery. He was the only son not to join the gang. In 1949 he was murdered by his wife.

"Ma" Kate Barker

THE BARKER GANG

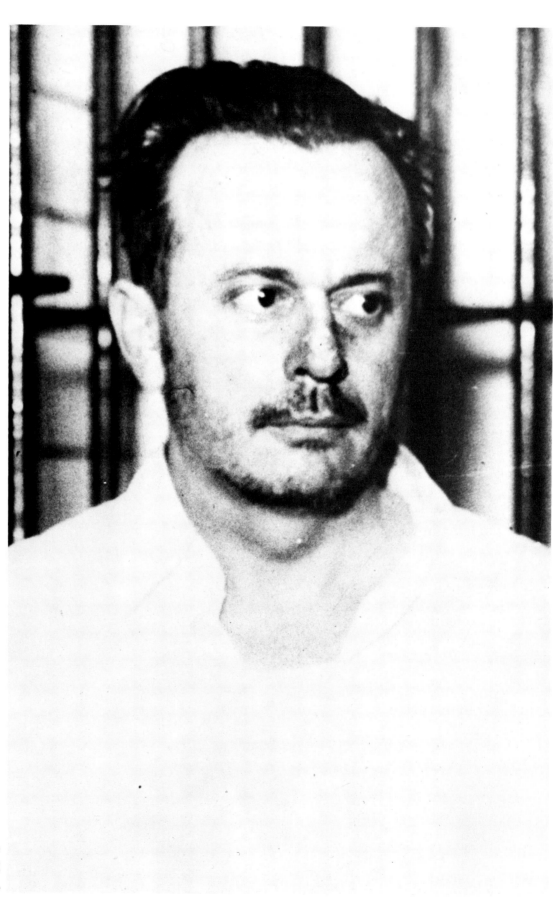

ST. PAUL, MINNESOTA, 1935 – Arthur "Doc" Barker

THE BARKER GANG

Fred Barker

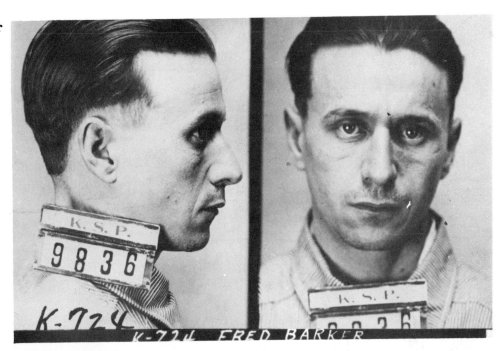

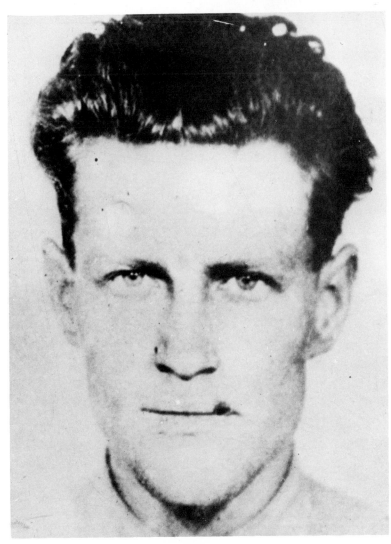

Volney Davis, machine gun operator for the Barker Gang

THE BARKER GANG

OKLAWAHA, FLORIDA, January 16, 1935 – Fred and "Ma" Barker's bungalow on Lake Weir where both were slain after a four-hour gun battle with FBI agents.

THE BARKER GANG

OKLAWAHA, FLORIDA, January 17, 1935 – The bodies of Fred Barker and his mother, "Ma" Barker, lie on slabs in the morgue after a fatal shoot-out. The Barkers hid out in this little Florida town for months before FBI agents learned of their whereabouts. Agents surrounded their bungalow and killed them as they attempted to shoot their way free.

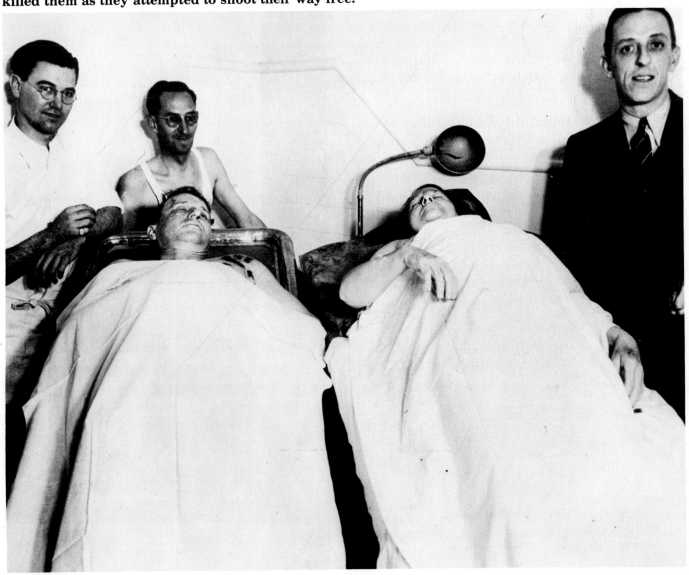

ALVIN "CREEPY" KARPIS

Alvin Karpis became a big time "thief", as he preferred to be called, when he teamed up with the Barkers in 1931. He remained with the gang until 1935 and was an integral part of their criminal activities for those four years. When the gang crumbled in 1935, Karpis managed to escape along with Harry Campbell.

Karpis and Campbell remained together, staying as far ahead of the law as they possibly could; on one occasion, just barely managing to elude the FBI in Atlantic City. In Hot Springs, Fred Hunter told them of a plan he had to steal the payroll of the Youngstown Sheet and Tube Plant, as the truck carrying the money passed through Warren, Ohio in April, 1935. Hunter remained behind for fear of being recognized in his home town of Warren, while Karpis and Campbell pulled off the robbery and returned $70,000 richer. FBI Director, J. Edgar Hoover, vowed to capture Karpis himself.

Karpis had something in mind that would really start Hoover's blood boiling: a train robbery. Carrying on a nostalgic love affair with the ghost of Jesse James, Karpis wanted to pull off a train robbery both for the money as well as the criminal aesthetics involved. His target was the $200,000 payroll on the Erie Train in Garrettsville, Ohio. In November, 1935 Karpis, Campbell, Hunter and two others held up the train, but there was only $34,000 on board.

A furious Hoover began a massive search for Karpis, and the two played cat and mouse until May, 1936, when Karpis and Hunter were surrounded by FBI agents in New Orleans. Flying in especially for the event, J. Edgar Hoover personally made the arrest. The glory of the moment was only partially marred when it was discovered that none of the agents had remembered to bring a set of handcuffs and the two fugitives had to be bound together with their own neck ties.

Alvin Karpis was sentenced to life imprisonment in 1936 but he was paroled and deported to Canada in 1969.

ST. PAUL, MINNESOTA, May 7, 1936 – Alvin Karpis in his jail cell. J. Edgar Hoover, Director of the FBI, considered him to be "Public Enemy Number One."

ALVIN "CREEPY" KARPIS

ST. PAUL, MINNESOTA, May, 1936 – J. Edgar Hoover (left) leads the way
as Karpis (manacled) is taken into Federal Court here after his capture
in New Orleans.

   (Years later, Karpis offered his view of the times: "It's an old practice
of the FBI to dress up the truth with lies that make them look more
clever and powerful than they are. The most obvious flaw in the FBI story
of my capture lies in Hoover's own character. He didn't lead the attack on
me. He hid until he was told the coast was clear. Then he came out
to reap the glory.")

ALVIN "CREEPY" KARPIS

ST. PAUL, MINNESOTA, May, 1936 – Fred Hunter, captured with Alvin Karpis in New Orleans

ST. PAUL, MINNESOTA, May 8, 1936 Harry Campbell (manacled) was brought here for questioning in the Bremer and Hamm kidnappings and other major crimes. Captured in Toledo, Ohio, he surrendered without resistance. He was held in the same record bail of $500,000 as his partner, Alvin Karpis.

"BABY FACE" NELSON

"Baby Face" Nelson, born Lester Gillis, stood 5 foot 4¾ inches tall, which had its disadvantages for a boy growing up on Chicago's tough South Side. While he had the face of a choir boy, he longed for a tough reputation and soon became a cold-blooded killer. "Baby Face" worked the rackets in Chicago for a while until his antics got on the nerves of some of his larger competitors who urged him to leave town, which he promptly did.

It might have been because of his size and looks that Nelson was so vicious but, whatever the reason, no one was safe when "Baby Face" ("Big George" to his face) became angered. Always in search of recognition, Nelson was furious when other gangs kept getting all the credit and publicity for crimes he had pulled off.

Nelson teamed up with John Dillinger right after the latter broke out of prison, and the usually sedate Dillinger robberies became bloodier affairs. They finally split up and after Dillinger was supposed to have been killed in Chicago, Nelson finally inherited a prominent place on the FBI wanted list. Consequently it seemed a good time to head out to the West Coast with his wife, Helen, and another gangster named John Chase.

Some nine months later, after returning to the Midwest, Nelson had a shoot out with two FBI agents on a country road, near Barrington, Illinois. Nelson killed the two agents and took seventeen slugs in return. His body was found the next day; he had been dumped out of the car naked by his wife and his friend.

1934 – "Baby Face" Nelson

DUTCH SCHULTZ

Dutch Schultz, born Arthur Flegenheimer, was a New York gangster in charge of bootlegging in the Bronx and parts of Manhattan from the mid-1920's to the mid-1930's. He was also involved in the policy game and slot machines. Ultimately, he was responsible for "Legs" Diamond's murder.

Thomas E. Dewey, then Special Prosecutor for New York City, began an all out scourge on gangland crime in 1935 and Schultz's policy rackets began suffering. When Dutch spread the word that he wanted to kill Dewey, he became an embarrassment for the New York gang chiefs Buchalter and Luciano who saw the folly in such a move. When Dutch refused to listen to reason, they had no other alternative but to turn him over to Albert Anastasia's Murder, Inc. execution team. Dutch was shot while having dinner in a Newark, New Jersey restaurant and died shortly after on October 23, 1935.

November, 1935 – Arthur "Dutch Schultz" Flegenheimer

DUTCH SCHULTZ

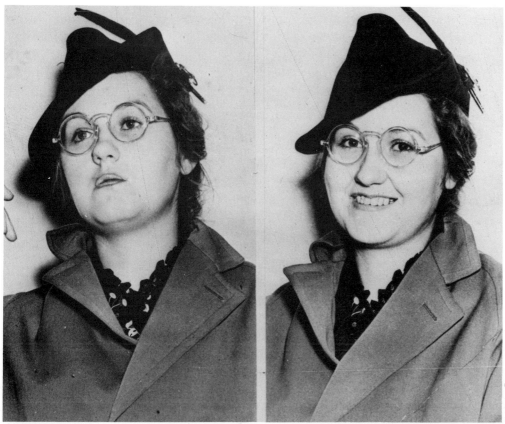

**Three faces of Mrs. Arthur
Flegenheimer, widow
of Dutch Schultz**

DUTCH SCHULTZ

SYRACUSE, NEW YORK, April 28, 1935 – Even a mistrial is a relief to Dutch Schultz. With his bail of Liberty Bonds continued, he walks from the court a temporarily free man, and stops to chat with George Castelman, a well-known character of Syracuse.

OPPOSITE PAGE: NEWARK, NEW JERSEY, October 23, 1935 – Dutch Schultz, mortally wounded while having dinner at the Palace Chophouse

THE MAFIA

Crime historians place the beginnings of the Mafia in the late 13th Century when Sicily was struggling to free itself from the domination of the French. A secret society was instrumental in the fight and their slogan was "Morte Alla Francia Italia Anela!" (Death to the French is Italy's Cry!) The word "mafia" is an acronym taken from the slogan.

The society remained benevolent until the 19th Century when criminals gained the upper hand. Not only did the criminal element gain control of the society, but the Mafia began spreading out all over Europe and the United States. The U.S. faction was viewed as a sort of black sheep due to the fact that it constantly resorted to murder as a solution to its problems.

American officials first became aware of the Mafia in 1890 when New Orleans Police Chief David Hennessey was shot and killed by the society which feared exposure through him. The Mafia has existed from that point on as an extremely powerful force in the United States, but it was not until the 1950's that the mafiosi gained complete control of the National Crime Syndicate.

The Mafia is an organization which, obviously, does not thrive on publicity, but the two most public expressions of its existence were Apalachin and Joseph Valachi. In November, 1957, the one hundred top mafiosi in America met in Apalachin, New York. State Police, acting on a tip, raided the estate of beer distributor Joseph Barbara and arrested numerous Mafia members. Apparently someone had taken issue with the impending election of Vito Genovese (a Neopolitan, not a Sicilian) as head of the entire Mafia.

Then in 1962, Joseph Valachi, a former Mafia member, turned informer and let the American public know for the first time the extent to which the Mafia controlled organized crime in the United States.

The Mafia bosses in the United States who maintained old world flair and manners were known as "mustache petes". Salvatore Maranzano was both the last of them and the founder of La Cosa Nostra.

Maranzano dreamt of becoming dictator of all the Mafia, the boss of bosses, and he actually succeeded – for a while. Maranzano went to war with "Joe the Boss" Masseria and dozens of mafiosi throughout the country were murdered. Eventually, "Lucky" Luciano and Vito Genovese decided to end what was called the Castellammarese War by having their boss Masseria murdered. They did and sued for peace.

What Maranzano wanted was an entire reorganization of the Mafia with himself at the top and various families beneath him. His pet name for the whole was La Cosa Nostra. Luciano and company feigned agreement, biding their time and looking for a way to murder Maranzano. Maranzano had his own suspicions about Luciano and his friends, so he hired "Mad Dog" Coll to murder them first. Luciano was faster, and Salvatore Maranzano was murdered in his New York office on September 10, 1931. He was gone but the structure he had built lived on after him.

PALERMO, SICILY – The eternal victim of Mafia violence is the woman of Sicily. Here, black-clad women weep hysterically for a relative who was the victim of a Mafia vendetta. They mourn at the spot in the hills near Palermo where their kinsman, a farmer, was slain by the "lupaba" (shotgun), a traditional Mafia weapon.

THE MAFIA

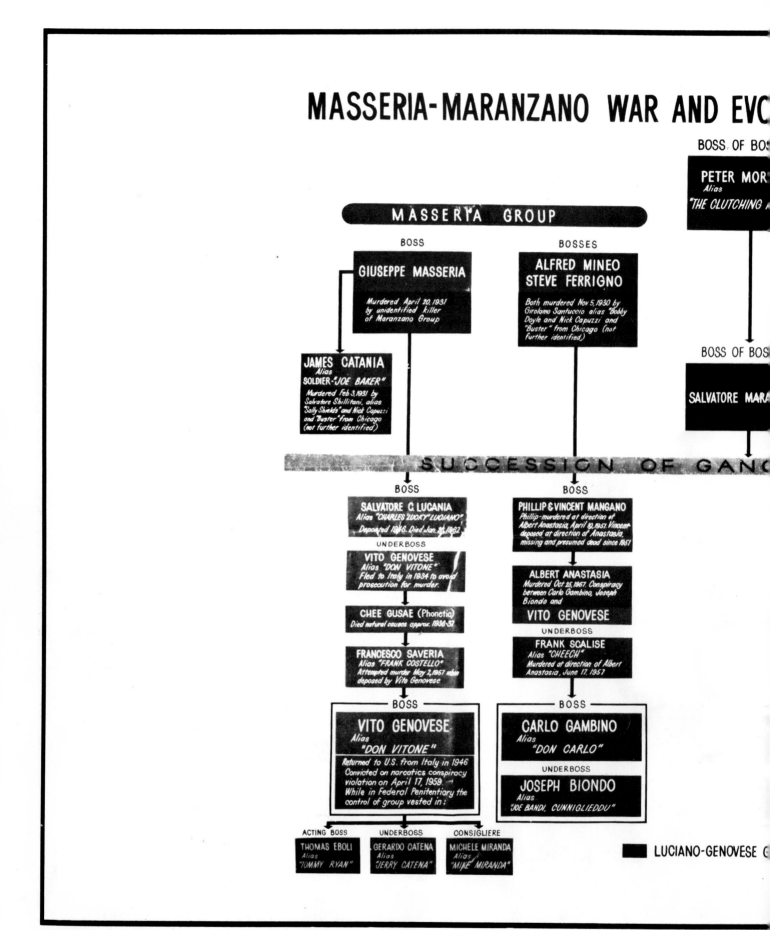

MASSERIA-MARANZANO WAR AND EVO

BOSS OF BOS

PETER MOR
Alias
"THE CLUTCHING

MASSERIA GROUP

BOSS

GIUSEPPE MASSERIA

*Murdered April 20, 1931
by unidentified killer
of Maranzano Group*

JAMES CATANIA
Alias
SOLDIER-"JOE BAKER"
*Murdered Feb 3, 1931 by
Salvatore Shillitani, alias
"Sally Shields" and Nick Capuzzi
and "Buster" from Chicago
(not further identified)*

BOSSES

**ALFRED MINEO
STEVE FERRIGNO**

*Both murdered Nov 5, 1930 by
Girolamo Santuccio alias "Bobby
Doyle and Nick Capuzzi and
"Buster" from Chicago (not
further identified)*

BOSS OF BOS

SALVATORE MARA

SUCCESSION OF GANG

BOSS

SALVATORE C LUCANIA
Alias "CHARLES "LUCKY" LUCIANO"
Deposed 1946. Died Jan 26, 1962

UNDERBOSS

VITO GENOVESE
*Alias "DON VITONE"
Fled to Italy in 1934 to avoid
prosecution for murder.*

CHEE GUSAE (Phonetic)
Died natural causes approx. 1936-37

FRANCESCO SAVERIA
*Alias "FRANK COSTELLO"
Attempted murder May 2, 1957 when
deposed by Vito Genovese*

BOSS

VITO GENOVESE
Alias
"DON VITONE"

*Returned to U.S. from Italy in 1946
Convicted on narcotics conspiracy
violation on April 17, 1959
While in Federal Penitentiary the
control of group vested in:*

BOSS

PHILLIP & VINCENT MANGANO
*Phillip murdered at direction of
Albert Anastasia, April 19, 1951. Vincent
deposed at direction of Anastasia,
missing and presumed dead since 1951*

ALBERT ANASTASIA
*Murdered Oct 25, 1957. Conspiracy
between Carlo Gambino, Joseph
Biondo and*
VITO GENOVESE

UNDERBOSS

FRANK SCALISE
*Alias "CHEECH"
Murdered at direction of Albert
Anastasia, June 17, 1957*

BOSS

CARLO GAMBINO
Alias
"DON CARLO"

UNDERBOSS

JOSEPH BIONDO
Alias
"JOE BANDI, CUNNIGLIEDDU"

ACTING BOSS	UNDERBOSS	CONSIGLIERE
THOMAS EBOLI *Alias* "TOMMY RYAN"	**GERARDO CATENA** *Alias* "JERRY CATENA"	**MICHELE MIRANDA** *Alias* "MIKE MIRANDA"

■ LUCIANO-GENOVESE G

**WASHINGTON, D.C., October 1, 1963 – This is a copy of the master chart
naming the leaders of New York's notorious "Five Families" which allegedly
dominate the rackets in the city of New York, as unveiled by Joseph Valachi
during his testimony before the Senate Investigations Subcommittee here.**

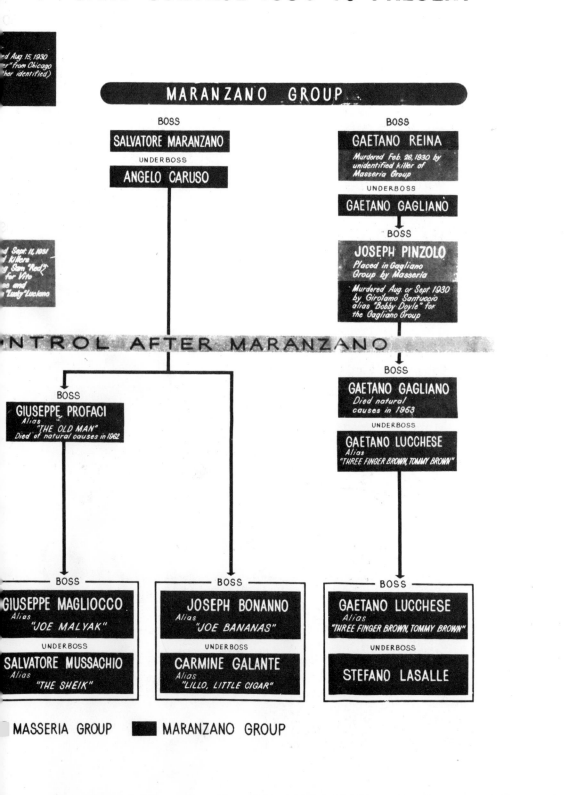

d Aug. 15, 1930
r" from Chicago
her identified)

MARANZANO GROUP

BOSS
SALVATORE MARANZANO
UNDERBOSS
ANGELO CARUSO

BOSS
GAETANO REINA
Murdered Feb. 26, 1930 by
unidentified killer of
Masseria Group
UNDERBOSS
GAETANO GAGLIANO

BOSS
JOSEPH PINZOLO
Placed in Gagliano
Group by Masseria
Murdered Aug. or Sept. 1930
by Girolamo Santuccio
alias "Bobby Doyle" for
the Gagliano Group

d Sept. 11, 1931
killers
g Sam "Red"?
for Vito
e and
"Lucky" Luciano

NTROL AFTER MARANZANO

BOSS
GIUSEPPE PROFACI
Alias
"THE OLD MAN"
Died of natural causes in 1962

BOSS
GAETANO GAGLIANO
Died natural
causes in 1953
UNDERBOSS
GAETANO LUCCHESE
Alias
"THREE FINGER BROWN, TOMMY BROWN"

BOSS
GIUSEPPE MAGLIOCCO
Alias
"JOE MALYAK"
UNDERBOSS
SALVATORE MUSSACHIO
Alias
"THE SHEIK"

BOSS
JOSEPH BONANNO
Alias
"JOE BANANAS"
UNDERBOSS
CARMINE GALANTE
Alias
"LILLO, LITTLE CIGAR"

BOSS
GAETANO LUCCHESE
Alias
"THREE FINGER BROWN, TOMMY BROWN"
UNDERBOSS
STEFANO LASALLE

☐ MASSERIA GROUP   ■ MARANZANO GROUP

"LUCKY" LUCIANO

Charles "Lucky" Luciano was one of the most powerful criminals America has ever had. He received his basic training with the Five Points Gang from New York's Lower East Side and apprenticed with Johnny Torrio until the latter left to join Al Capone. Luciano remained in New York and became a member of the Masseria family where he took over prostitution. "Lucky" and his men sold protection to the madams and their girls, and the ones who didn't buy ended up with broken legs or worse. Luciano collected fifty percent from every madam and by 1927 he was a millionaire in control of most of the whores in Manhattan.

In 1930 war broke out between the Maranzano and Masseria families. A particularly bloody affair, Luciano felt he could save a lot of his men and further his own cause by having his boss, "Joe the Boss" Masseria murdered. This was done on April 15, 1931, with Luciano personally setting up the hit, and the gangland war was over. Months later Luciano had the opposing Mafia head, Maranzano, murdered and took charge of the city.

In 1934 Luciano formed the National Crime Syndicate with Meyer Lansky, Louis "Lepke" Buchalter, Joe Adonis and a number of others. The Syndicate ordered Dutch Schultz murdered when he wanted to do away with Special Prosecutor Thomas E. Dewey, and with seeming ingratitude, Dewey immediately went after Luciano. The police pressured prostitutes until in 1936 they had enough to convict him of extortion and of directing prostitution rings.

Luciano's power apparently did not diminish in prison and when the United States became embroiled in World War II, he reputedly provided information and assistance that contributed to the success of the Allied landing on Sicily.

Three years later in return for his help, Luciano was released from prison but on the condition that he be deported to Italy. By 1947 Luciano was back in Havana, helping to direct the Syndicate operations in the States. Eventually expelled from Cuba, he returned to Italy where he continued to engage in various illicit activities, notably narcotics. The Italian authorities banned him from Rome, but what effect that had on curtailing his activities is not known. Luciano died of a heart attack in 1962.

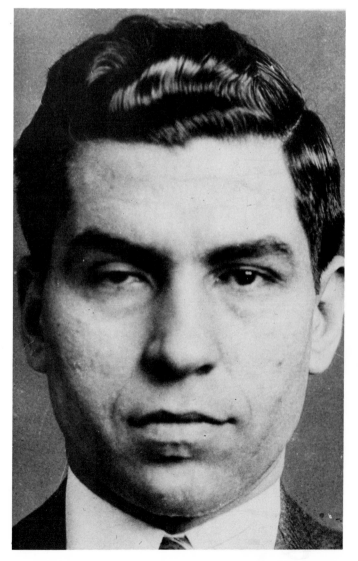

1935 – Charles "Lucky" Luciano

"LUCKY" LUCIANO

HAVANA, February 24, 1947 – "Lucky" Luciano, former New York vice overlord, is pictured after his arrest in Havana. With him are Benito Herrera (left), head of the Cuban Secret Police, and Alfredo Pequeno, Minister of Interior. Luciano faces deportation on charges of perjury.

"LUCKY" LUCIANO

ROME, 1949 – Above: "Lucky"
Luciano at a private house party in Rome.

Luciano dancing with an unidentified
woman at the same party.

"LUCKY" LUCIANO

NAPLES, ITALY, November 27, 1954 – "Lucky" Luciano, a home-loving, elegant (note smoking jacket), scholarly (note rimless specs) gentleman, spends an evening at home with his mistress, Igea Lissoni, and their dog. The former vice and narcotics racketeer hasn't got much choice in the matter as the police slapped a curfew on him and he must stay at home. "Lucky" also has to find a job, stay in a 16 mile radius of Naples, keep out of bars, and stay away from "questionable" associates. Says "Lucky", "I'm innocent as a lamb. Maybe I would be a good bookkeeper. You know I can count money."

VITO GENOVESE

Vito "Don Vito" Genovese and "Lucky" Luciano became partners in crime in 1917, pulling off small-time burglaries. They both joined "Joe the Boss" Masseria's gang and it was Genovese along with three others who shot and killed Masseria in 1931 to end gangland's Castellammarese war. Soon after, Genovese and Luciano continued their partnership by forming the National Crime Syndicate. The two had been together some seventeen years and Vito's share of the take from their vice and narcotics operations had been estimated at $200,000 a year.

Fearing a murder rap, Genovese fled to Italy in 1937 where he worked his way into Mussolini's good graces by donating some $25,000 to the Fascist party – the party which had sworn to wipe out the Mafia.

In 1944 Genovese managed to secure an interpreter's position with U.S. Military Intelligence. He apparently was considered invaluable by the Americans for exposing a large number of black market operatives in southern Italy. Authorities later found out, however, that Genovese was simply taking over their operations once he had denounced the black marketeers. The Army discovered that Genovese had fled a murder indictment in the States in 1935, so he was arrested and brought back for trial in the U.S. By having one of the witnesses against him murdered, Vito once again retained his freedom for lack of evidence.

Genovese then set about rebuilding his Mafia empire by killing off the newly ensconced chiefs. First to go was Willie Moretti in 1951, followed by Steve Franse in 1953 and Albert Anastasia in 1957. He also frightened Frank Costello into early retirement. Later that same year, Genovese had himself named boss of bosses by the one hundred most important Mafia members

NEW YORK, July 8, 1958 – Vito Genovese is shown talking to reporters after his release here on $50,000 bail on an indictment which charges him and thirty-six other persons with conspiring to import and sell narcotics.

throughout the U.S. This was the famous Apalachin meeting which was broken up by New York State Police shortly after its start.

In 1958 the government had collected enough evidence against "Don Vito" to send him to prison for fifteen years on a narcotics charge. Genovese went, but he ordered murders and directed Mafia activities from his cell until his death in 1969.

VITO GENOVESE

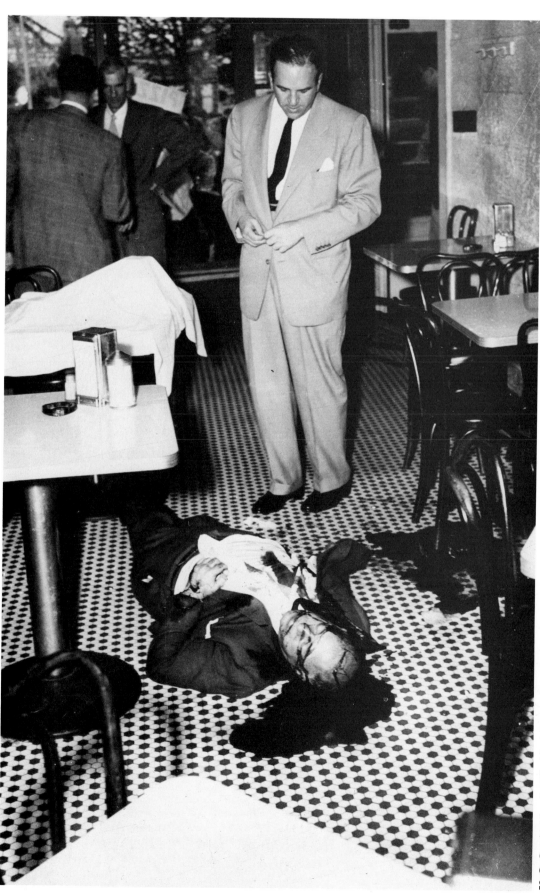

CLIFFSIDE PARK, NEW JERSEY, October 4, 1951 – Racketeer Willie Moretti lies in his own blood after being shot to death at Joe's Restaurant. The 57-year-old gambler was a long-time friend of rackets kingpin Joe Adonis. Moretti's brother, Salvatore, was known to be Adonis's lieutenant. Looking down at the body is Bergen County Attorney General Nelson Stamler.

"TRIGGER MIKE" COPPOLA

Mike Coppola took over from Vito Genovese in 1937 when the mobster fled to Italy, and it has been estimated that Coppola earned some $1,000,000 yearly through the rackets he inherited from Genovese.

He was allegedly responsible for the death of his first wife, Doris (shown here with Coppola on the left and her father on the right), after she had the misfortune of overhearing his plans for the murder of a New York politician. She died the day after she gave birth to a baby girl and it was his second wife who later accused him of having done away with Doris.

The second Mrs. Coppola was physically and mentally abused to the degree that she eventually testified against him in 1961. She later committed suicide in Rome in 1962, while Coppola died of natural causes in 1966.

"BUGSY" SIEGEL

Benjamin "Bugsy" Siegel belonged to the same crowd as "Lucky" Luciano and Joe Adonis, and he was one of the four men who murdered "Joe the Boss" Masseria. He had good Mafia credentials, and they rewarded his sincerity and loyalty by financing his move to the West Coast to consolidate the Brotherhood's operations. Siegel was reportedly given a half-million dollars to start his business.

The gangster hobnobbed with Hollywood celebrities including Jean Harlow, Cary Grant, Clark Gable, and his old friend George Raft. He was obsessed with "class" and what he considered straight contacts. His mistresses even included a countess with whom he tried to sell explosives to Mussolini.

Siegel's real business was running the rackets and narcotics on the West Coast, along with a sideline of delivering racing results to the East Coast bookies. It was Siegel's dream to set up a legal gambling paradise in Las Vegas, the construction of which he began in 1945. Siegel's Flamingo Club (the nickname of his mistress, Virginia Hill) was one of the first truly posh gambling resorts to be built in Las Vegas, but his career was cut short when he refused to follow an order from Luciano to return the $3,000,000 the Syndicate had pumped into his hotel.

"Bugsy" paid his debt with his life. He was shot and killed at the home of Virginia Hill on June 20, 1947.

Benjamin "Bugsy" Siegel

"BUGSY" SIEGEL

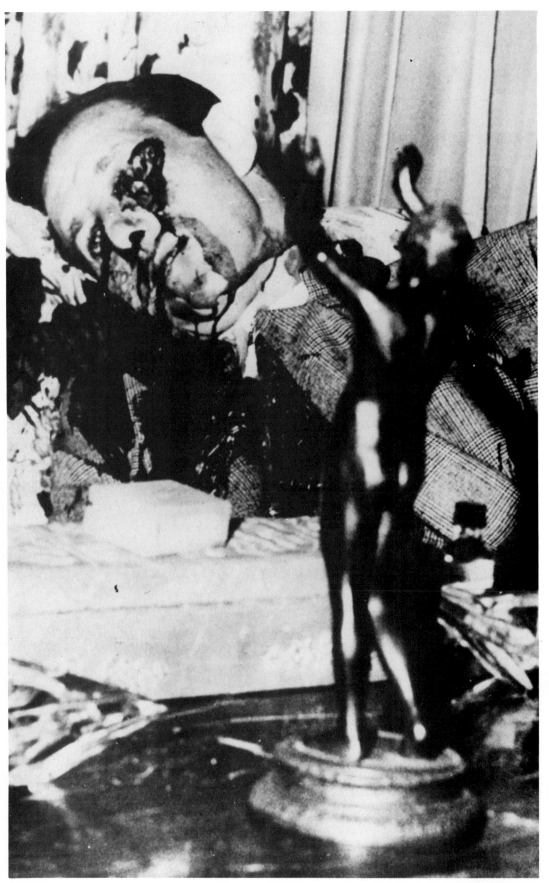

BEVERLY HILLS, CALIFORNIA, June 21,1947 – "Bugsy" Siegel, 42, part owner of the $5 million Flamingo Club in Las Vegas and underworld big shot, was shot down shortly before midnight, June 20 by a gunman who fired a burst of nine shots through the window of the swank Beverly Hills home of Virginia Hill, Siegel's mistress. "Bugsy", named several years ago in connection with Murder, Inc., was seated on a couch reading a newspaper with Allen Smiley, Hollywood sporting figure, when the bullets crashed through the window and found their mark.

FRANK COSTELLO

NEW YORK, March 14, 1951 – Frank Costello, reputed prime minister of the underworld, fidgets with glasses, chin and eyelids in these studies made during his appearance before the Kefauver Senate Crime Committee in a New York Federal Court. When he refused to be televised during the hearing, the video cameras trained on his arms and hands and an unusual television show ensued, betraying the nervous strain and anxiety of the calm-surfaced Costello. In a February hearing, the Committee reported that Costello and Joe Adonis were the leaders of one of the two major crime syndicates in the U.S. The other syndicate is headed by the Capone gangs. Charles "Lucky" Luciano, deported from this country and now residing in Rome, was termed the referee between the two groups.

JOE ADONIS

NEW YORK, January 3, 1956 – Joe Adonis, the 53-year-old syndicate racketeer, is seen in his cabin aboard the Italian Liner *Conte Biancamano* as he prepares to sail for Italy. He chose exile over jail after being convicted of gambling and perjury – the government had been trying to deport him as an "undesirable" since 1948. Adonis was one of the men who rose very rapidly after the formation of the National Crime Syndicate in 1934. He specialized in hijacking and gambling, and held a position on the board of the Syndicate for twenty years. In the 1940's Adonis came to be in control of most of the rackets in the state of New Jersey.

PAUL "THE WAITER" RICCA

CHICAGO, June 10, 1957 – Paul "The Waiter" Ricca, who had his citizenship revoked after the court ruled he had entered the U.S. illegally, today won a delay on charges of income tax evasion. Ricca is shown gleefully clapping his hands as he leaves Federal Court with his attorney. The government contended that the evidence "clearly established that this defendant is the Paul de Lucia to whom a certificate of naturalization was granted and that he used a false name when he applied for citizenship."

Ricca was a Chicago gangster who had worked for Al Capone. After Capone went to jail, Ricca stayed on under the mob's new chief, Frank Nitti. If Nitti was the titular head, Ricca was considered to be the brains. For this reason, when the Syndicate was formed in 1934, Ricca, without Nitti's knowledge, was chosen to head up the Chicago operation. In the late 1940's, Ricca took over complete control of Chicago and held it until his death in 1972, after which Tony Accardo took over.

"BIG FRENCH" DEMANGE

"Big French" De Mange, chief enforcer for New York bootlegger, Owen "Owney" Madden

THE DRAGNA FAMILY

CALIFORNIA, 1950 – Police rounded up these five men and booked them on charges of suspicion of conspiracy to commit murder as a result of the bombing of mobster Mickey Cohen.

Left to right: Louis Dragna, 29; Tom Dragna, 61; Frank Dragna, 26; Guilermo Adamo, 54; and Paul Dragna, 28. (Jack Dragna, the mob's leader, is not shown.)

The Dragna family head the West Coast bookmaking racket and are said to be working under direct orders from the Mafia.

RAYMOND PATRIARCA

Involved in vice, gambling and loan sharking during the 1940's and 50's, Raymond Patriarca was careful to avoid any incriminating links with the crime organization he controlled. Joe Valachi, in his statements to the Justice Department, named Patriarca, "The Padrone", as chief of New England's Mafia. Convicted on murder conspiracy charges in 1968, Patriarca began serving his sentence in 1970. It is said that, even from prison, he still controls the New England syndicate.

JOHNNY DIO

WASHINGTON, August 8, 1957 – Infuriated hoodlum Johnny Dio glares angrily at the camera after slugging UPI photographer Stanley Tretick (left) who ducks away. The mobster threw his punch after being ordered from the Senate hearing room by Rackets Committee Chairman Senator John McClellan (Democrat from Arkansas), because of the hubbub which arose when Dio strode in. Dio had been called to testify on his alleged leadership of labor racketeering in New York.

MICHAEL MIRANDA

NEW YORK, May 21, 1959 – Michael Miranda steps out of a car in front of Federal Court here after being picked up in a nationwide roundup of big-name racketeers. He and twenty-six others were indicted by a Federal grand jury in New York on charges of conspiring to obstruct justice by refusing to say what went on at the Apalachin, New York crime convention in 1957.

THE GALLO BROTHERS

BROOKLYN, NEW YORK, October 10, 1961 – Joey Gallo (left) and his brother Larry (right) walk out of Kings County Court en route to jail and protective custody. Police found Larry and other Gallo henchmen hiding out with deadly weapons in two apartments, while Joey was picked up in Greenwich Village. "It seems quite clear that they were banding together for safety in fear of execution by a rival mob," said District Attorney Edward Silver.

THE GALLO BROTHERS

NEW YORK – Larry Gallo after learning of his brother Joey's death at Umberto's Clam House in New York's Little Italy

JOSEPH "JOE BANANAS" BONANNO

NEW YORK, June 21, 1966 – "Joe Bananas" looks straight ahead as he arrives for a hearing at Federal Court on charges of obstructing justice. The alleged Cosa Nostra boss disappeared in October, 1964, not returning to public sight until last month.

MEYER LANSKY

In the early 1930's, Meyer Lansky (often called the financial wizard of the underworld) and "Lucky" Luciano were instrumental in forming what has come to be known as the Syndicate. The Syndicate was established to put some law and order into this nation's disorganized criminal life. An organization of this size and importance logically required an enforcement arm to tame unruly members or to suppress those who might think of becoming independent. This enforcement arm was dubbed Murder, Inc.

It had leaders like "Bugsy" Siegel, Louis "Lepke" Buchalter, and Albert Anastasia, and killers like Abe "Kid Twist" Reles, Frank "The Dasher" Abbandando, "Happy" Maione, "Blue Jaw" Magoon, and the most notorious of all, Harry Strauss, better known as "Pittsburgh Phil" (reputed to have murdered five hundred people from the late 1920's to 1940).

The organization was almost perfect. Killers would get "contracts" to "hit" "bums", and since the executioners frequently came from out of town, there was little opportunity for the victim to defend himself.

In the spring of 1940 Murder, Inc. was dealt a severe blow when Reles turned informer, telling all he could remember. Heads rolled, and eventually so did Reles's. While waiting to testify, he was guarded by three shifts of six policemen each in a Brooklyn hotel, and still managed to leave the premises from a sixth floor window on November 21, 1941. Strong evidence would indicate that he was pushed from the hotel room window and died, not surprisingly, upon impact.

Based on Reles's testimony, "Mendy" Weiss, Louis Capone, "Happy" Maione, Frank Abbandando, and Harry Strauss were all executed.

Meyer Lansky

MEYER LANSKY

MIAMI, February 28, 1973 – Leaving the courthouse for lunch,
Meyer Lansky has a ready smile for photographers.

MEYER LANSKY

MIAMI, December 6, 1974 – Meyer Lansky (right), shown here with his attorney E. David Rose in 1973, has won his freedom from the courts. The Federal Government decided today to give up its long, tedious fight to put the 72-year-old organized crime legend behind bars.

MURDER, INC.

BROOKLYN, NEW YORK, August 7, 1940 – Harry "Pittsburgh Phil" Strauss,
in a cell after he was arraigned on a murder charge for the 1935 shotgun
slaying of Abraham Meer. Strauss was one of the mob syndicate's chief
contract killers.

MURDER, INC.

NEW YORK, August 25, 1939 – Louis "Lepke" Buchalter, shown in an F.B.I. mug shot after the powerful garment racketeer surrendered to J. Edgar Hoover, F.B.I. Director, in New York following a nationwide search for him

Louis "Lepke" Buchalter

MURDER, INC.

ALBANY, NEW YORK, July 20, 1943 – The death sentence was pronounced for the second time today upon Louis "Lepke" Buchalter (center), and two members of his gang, Emmanuel "Mendy" Weiss and Louis Capone. They were condemned to die in the electric chair the week of September 15. Buchalter is shown here arriving from the New York City Federal House of Detention to hear his sentence. Guarding him with a submachine gun is Albany Detective Joseph Nowak.

BROOKLYN, NEW YORK, March 20, 1949 – Three alleged chiefs of Brooklyn murder syndicate hide their faces while being indicted. Left to right: Frank "The Dasher" Abbandando, Harry "Happy" Maione, and Harry "Pittsburgh Phil" Strauss.

BROOKLYN, NEW YORK, May 8, 1940 – "Happy" Maione (left) and Frank "The Dasher" Abbandando, in court as their trial began

MURDER, INC.

Abe "Kid Twist" Reles turned informer on many Organization contract killers and went out the window of a Brooklyn hotel while waiting under heavy guard to testify. His death has never been proven to have been of his own accord.

MURDER, INC.

NEW YORK, March 26, 1940 – Albert Tannenbaum, 34, indicted for the murder of Irving Ashmenas, a Dewey witness, is pictured here in District Attorney O'Dwyer's office where he was questioned in the investigation of the Brooklyn murder syndicate.

PHILADELPHIA, June 30, 1953 – Jack "The Dandy" Parisi, alleged Murder, Inc. executioner, talks to his wife, Theresa, during his deportation hearings. Parisi, who had ignored his wife for ten years, threatened that she would suffer if he were sent to Italy.

MURDER, INC.

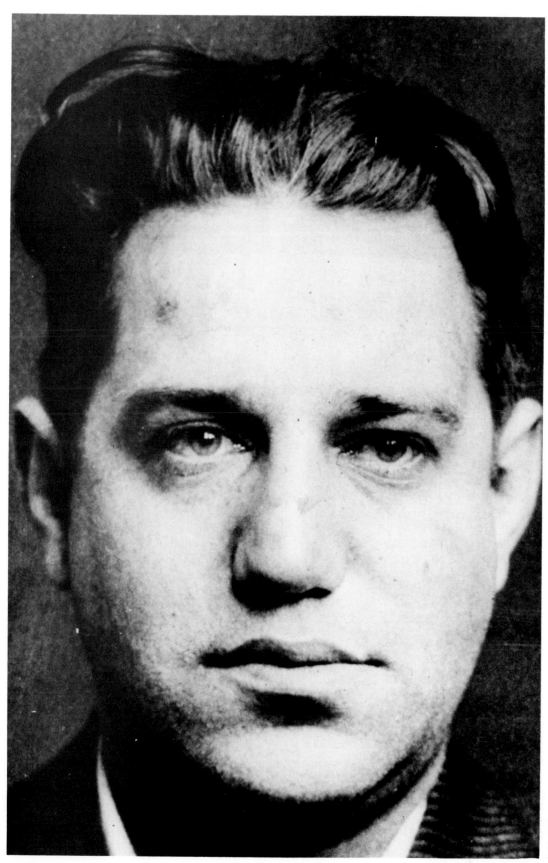

Seymour "Blue Jaw"
Magoon, Murder,
Inc. executioner

ALBERT ANASTASIA

Albert Anastasia got his start in organized crime with the Masseria family and was an intimate of "Lucky" Luciano, "Bugsy" Siegel, Meyer Lansky, Vito Genovese, and Joe Adonis. Anastasia, along with Genovese, Adonis, and Siegel, murdered "Joe the Boss" Masseria on the instructions of Luciano. After Luciano had Salvatore Maranzano killed, Anastasia's stock rose through association with his boss. Anastasia became "Lord High Executioner" or the head of Murder, Inc., after Abe "Kid Twist" Reles had virtually destroyed the outfit.

Anastasia was a ruthless murderer who seemingly killed for the joy of it. He once ordered the execution of a civilian named Arnold Schuster simply because the man had informed police that he had seen bankrobber Willie Sutton.

In the 1950's, Anastasia, already head of a Mafia family, incurred Vito Genovese's wrath. Anastasia was an ally of powerful syndicate boss Frank Costello, but after Costello began losing control, the head of Murder, Inc. became vulnerable. Anastasia was shot to death on Genovese's orders in a New York hotel barbershop on October 25, 1957. It was strongly rumored but never proven that Joey Gallo was involved in the Anastasia execution.

1932 – Albert Anastasia

ALBERT ANASTASIA

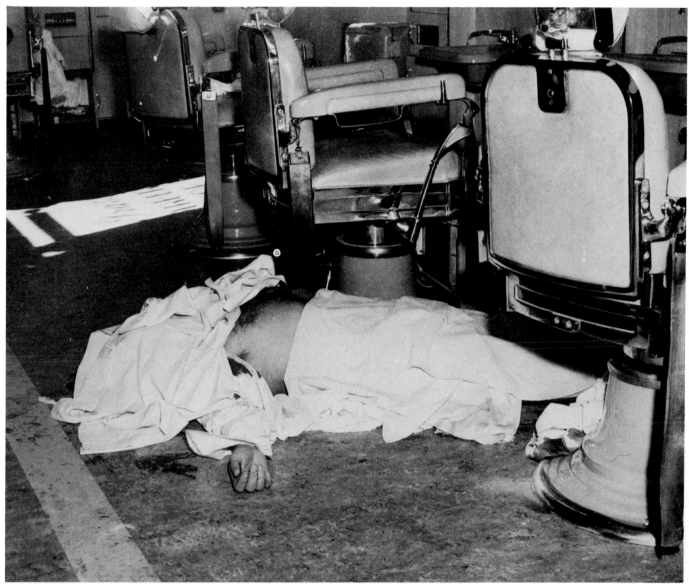

NEW YORK, October 25, 1957 – The body of Albert Anastasia, notorious gangland figure, is shown on the floor of the Park Sheraton Hotel (7th Avenue and 55th Street) near a barber chair he was preparing to sit in when he was shot and killed today. The daring daylight murder occurred at about 10:20 A.M. when, police were told, two masked men walked in swiftly, warned everyone to stand out of the way and opened fire at the man once called America's worst criminal.

JOE VALACHI

Joseph Valachi was never a very important member of the Cosa Nostra, but he is memorable because he was one of the few Mafia members to break the organization's code of *omerta* or silence.

Valachi had worked for Salvatore Maranzano until his death, and then for the Luciano family. He was an enforcer, numbers runner, and narcotics peddlar until 1959, when he was sentenced to fifteen years in Atlanta, Georgia for violation of narcotics laws.

Vito Genovese was also inhabiting a cell in Atlanta and was still one of the most powerful gangsters in the country. Genovese hated Valachi, who became justifiably fearful for his life. In 1962 Valachi killed John Saupp, a fellow inmate, who he mistakenly thought was going to kill him on Genovese's orders. Saupp being the wrong man, Valachi decided to turn informer and get federal protection.

For months on end, Valachi told the Senate Investigations Subcommittee everything he knew. The information wasn't entirely unknown, but served to corroborate much that had been rumored. Obviously the publicity was devestating for other mafiosi. Valachi died of a heart attack in 1971 in La Tuna Federal Prison, Texas.

1963 – Joe Valachi

TOP: **WASHINGTON, D.C., October 9, 1963 – Surrounded by a "platoon" of security agents, Joseph Valachi arrives at the Senate Caucus Room to resume his testimony before the Senate Investigations Subcommittee. Because of anonymous threats on Valachi's life, received by** the F.B.I., security precautions were increased around the underworld defector. Spectators were carefully screened.

BOTTOM: **Valachi (right) conferring with Levern Duffy, Assistant Counsel of the subcommittee**

JOE VALACHI

WASHINGTON, D.C., September 27, 1963 – General view of the Senate Caucus taken facing Joseph Valachi. Committee Chairman Senator John McClellan (back to camera) is presiding.

THE MURDER OF LEON TROTSKY

Leon Trotsky, the Russian revolutionary leader, lived in exile in a fortress-like villa in a suburb of Mexico City. He allowed very few people to see him for fear of assassination. In August, 1940 security at the villa was even tighter than usual since twenty men had attempted to kill the aging Trotsky several months earlier on May 24.

However one man, Jacques Mornard, known to Trotsky as Frank Jacson, had access to him and had been seeing him regularly as a trusted associate since four days after the attempted murder. On August 20, Jacson went to the Trotsky villa on the pretext of discussing a forthcoming magazine article. Once alone with him, Jacson pulled out a pickax which he drove into Leon Trotsky's head. Guards swarmed in immediately and captured Jacson, but it was too late for Trotsky who was mortally wounded and died shortly after.

Jacson was sentenced to twenty years in prison, the maximum allowed by Mexican law. As to his real identity, Jacson, alias Jacques Mornard, was apparently one Ramon Mercades del Rio, a Spaniard who had fought against Franco. Del Rio's mother had fled to the Soviet Union after the Spanish Civil War and had worked for the Soviet Secret Police. Upon his release in 1960, del Rio was issued a Czechoslovakian passport.

MEXICO CITY, August 23, 1940 – Leon Trotsky, just after death came in a Mexico City hospital

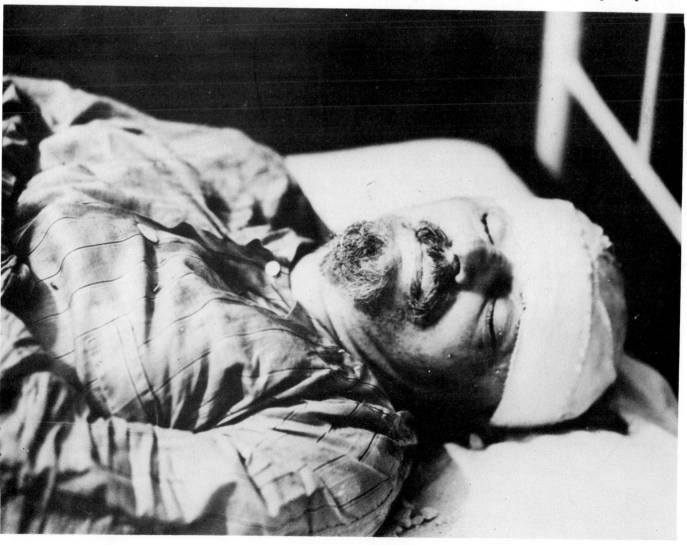

THE MURDER OF LEON TROTSKY

MEXICO CITY, August, 1940 – General Jose Manuel Nunez, Mexico City Chief of Police, pulls a dagger from the coat worn by Jacques Mornard.

Nunez holds the small pickax used by Mornard to inflict the head wounds responsible for the death of Leon Trotsky.

THE MURDER OF LEON TROTSKY

**MEXICO CITY, August 20, 1940 – Scene of the attack on Leon Trotsky
in his Mexico City villa**

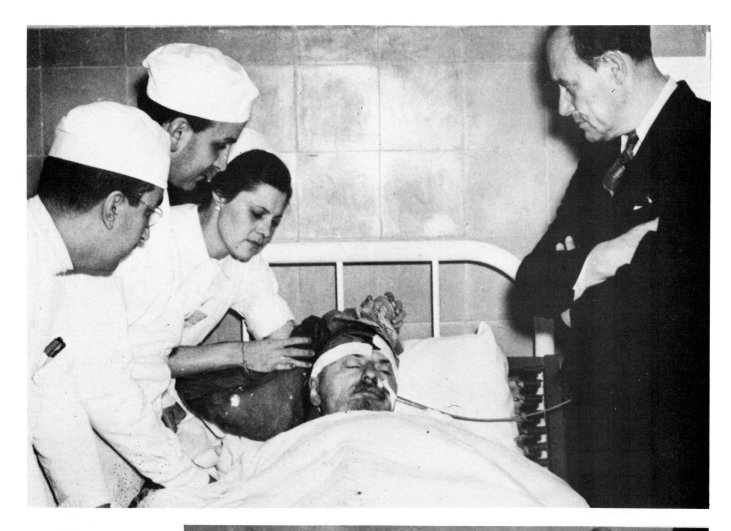

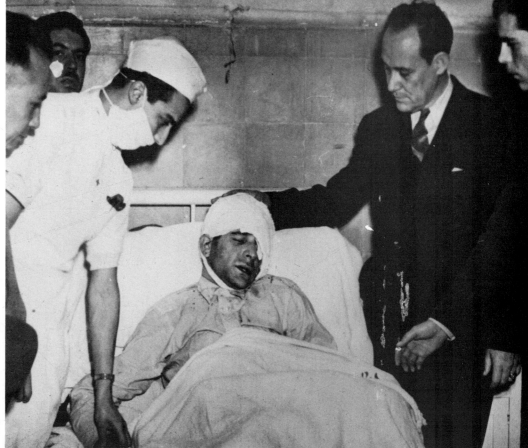

TOP: **MEXICO CITY, August 22, 1940 –** Leon Trotsky shown in his hospital bed the day before he died.
RIGHT: **Jacques Mornard,** recovering in the same hospital from a beating by Leon Trotsky's guards, suffered after he wounded the exiled Russian revolutionist with a pickax.

TOP: **MEXICO CITY, December 18, 1953 –** Dressed in a plain business suit instead of the regulation prison garb, Jacques Mornard, the pickax slayer of Leon Trotsky, indicated that he prefers the "safety" of his prison machine shop to a parole.

Mornard will become eligible for parole December 20, having completed two thirds of his twenty-year prison sentence. Authorities are convinced that friends of the murdered Trotsky and agents of the Soviet Regime, who are anxious to seal Mornard's lips permanently, are waiting to assassinate him if he steps through the prison gates.

BOTTOM: **MEXICO CITY, September 24, 1940 –** Crowds lining a street watch the funeral procession of Leon Trotsky en route to the cemetery. Interment plans remain uncertain; Trotsky's associates hoped to take the body to New York for a public funeral and then cremation, whereupon the ashes would be returned to Mexico.

HANS VAN MEEGEREN

After the Second World War, security specialists all over Western Europe sought people who had collaborated with the Nazis and their puppet governments. In Holland, one of the people accused of collaboration was an artist named Hans Van Meegeren.

Van Meegeren, it was alleged, had conspired with others to sell Nazi leader Göring a painting by Vermeer entitled "The Woman Taken in Adultery." Van Meegeren denied the charges of collaboration and stated that he himself had actually painted the picture sold to Göring. Not only that, he had forged five other Vermeers as well as two paintings by De Hoogh. No one believed Van Meegeren, and it is little wonder since a great number of reputations were at stake.

The courts decided to have the paintings appraised and the scientific tests proved that Van Meegeren had not lied. Van Meegeren was in the middle of committing another forgery to make certain that people believed him, when he learned that the collaboration charge had been dropped and one of forgery substituted.

Van Meegeren was sentenced to a year in prison, where he died at the age of 58. The one satisfying note of the affair is that Göring is reported to have paid 165,000 British pounds for his false Vermeer. But then again, the money might have been forged as well.

AMSTERDAM, November 5, 1945 – Hans Van Meegeren, 56-year-old Dutch artist, is shown at work on his painting, a perfect copy of Vermeer's "Jesus Teaching in the Temple", which cleared him of collaboration charges but unveiled the world's biggest art hoax. Van Meegeren was suspected of being a collaborationist after the liberation of Amsterdam because of the huge sums of money he possessed. With experts hired to watch him, he proved his claim to the extent, in this particular case, of "out-mastering" the old master. He finished this painting in two months in the presence of six witnesses.

WILLIAM HEIRENS

William Heirens suffered from sexual problems at a very early age. He would dress up in women's clothing and stare at pictures of Nazi leaders for hours on end. He apparently found sexual release through burglary. At the age of 13 he was arrested for carrying a loaded pistol and, upon searching the Heirens home, police found a sizeable arsenal.

Sent to a juvenile corrections institution, Heirens later proved himself a brilliant student and entered the University of Chicago, Leopold and Loeb's alma mater, as a sophomore. Unfortunately Heirens graduated from burglary to murder during this same period, when on June 3, 1945 he slashed the throat of Mrs. Josephine Ross. The next murder victim was Francis Brown on December 10. Then came his darkest crime.

On January 7, 1946 Heirens abducted, murdered and cut to pieces six-year-old Suzanne Degnan. Only hours after the murder he went about stuffing parts of her body into Chicago sewers. Heirens knew he was disturbed and after the murder of Miss Brown, he left an inscription begging police to catch him before he murdered again. On June 26, 1946 the police caught up with him. Heirens first blamed Suzanne's murder on a man named George Murman, who turned out to be none other than Heiren's nefarious alter ego.

Heirens was sentenced to three consecutive terms of life imprisonment.

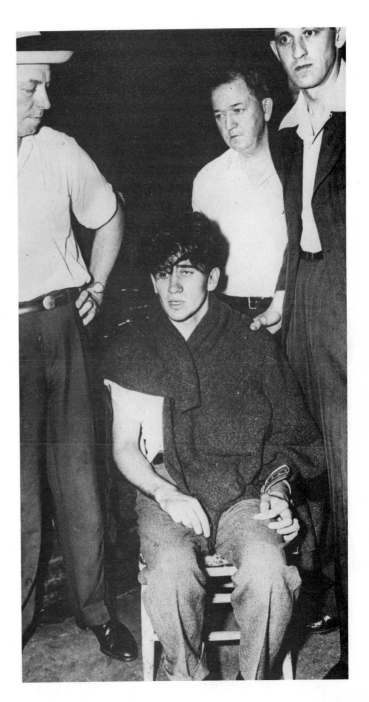

1946 – William Heirens

WILLIAM HEIRENS

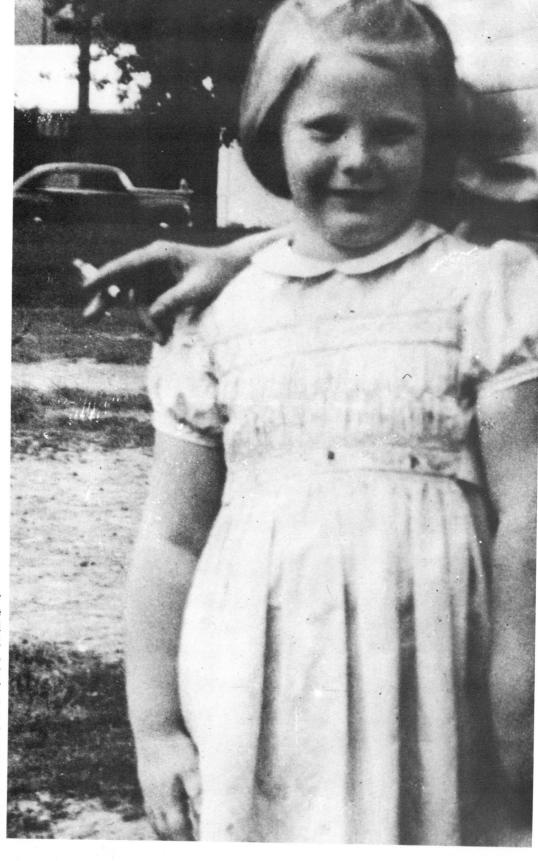

CHICAGO, January 8, 1946 – Suzanne Degnan, 6-year-old daughter of Mr. and Mrs. James Degnan, was brutally murdered after being kidnapped from her home yesterday. Her butchered body was discovered in a sewer and examination revealed that she had been choked to death by her kidnapper.

WILLIAM HEIRENS

1946 – Mr. and Mrs. George Heirens, parents of William

CHICAGO, January 8, 1946 – "Tell the kind people there is nothing they can do for us now but pray for us." These were the words of James E. Degnan (far right), father of Suzanne Degnan, seated with his wife (center), his brother, and Mrs. Degnan's sister.

WILLIAM HEIRENS

JOLIET, ILLINOIS, June 6, 1967 – Stateville Prison inmate is counseled by William Heirens (left) about a college course offered in the prison. Heirens, 38, who was sentenced in 1946 to three consecutive life terms for the murders of Suzanne Degnan and two women, now acts as an assistant to the superintendent of education of Stateville Prison. Warden Frank Pate said that Heirens has done a big job in helping him evaluate and revise the school's structure.

THE DURBAN CASTLE AFFAIR

James Camb was a 31-year-old deck-steward aboard the liner *Durban Castle*. In October, 1947 the ship was sailing from South Africa to England, and one of the passengers was Eileen Gibson, a 21-year-old actress. On October 18, eight days after setting sail from Johannesburg, Miss Gibson was reported missing. Camb had been spotted at her cabin door at 3 A.M. on the same morning. He also had scratches on both arms.

When the *Durban Castle* put in to Southhampton, Camb was taken by police and, after being told that any reasonable explanation of the girl's fate might be helpful, stated that she had met him at the cabin door wearing only a dressing gown. They had then had intercourse, during which she had been overcome by a seizure and died. The deck-steward reported that he had become panic-stricken and had pushed her through the porthole and into the sea.

The evidence was thought to weigh heavily against Camb, particularly since the marks on his arms appeared to have been inflicted in self-defense. Urine and blood marks found on the sheets, it was stated, could have been induced either by a seizure or by strangulation. The girl's pyjamas were missing from her cabin, which might indicate foul play or a lack of modesty on her part.

On March 23, 1948 Camb was found guilty of murder. He was released from prison in September, 1959.

1947 – James Camb, 31-year-old deck-steward on the liner *Durban Castle*

THE LONELY HEARTS KILLERS

Martha Beck, a nurse and the head of a school for crippled children in Florida, was extremely fat and had been so since childhood. Apparently her weight created a certain psychological sexual retardation.

In November, 1947, she received a letter from one Raymond Fernandez through a lonely hearts club. Fernandez was a professional fortune hunter and con man, who operated through such clubs. They met, but Fernandez left Martha after two days when he realized she had no money. Hurt and rejected, Martha attempted suicide, after sending a farewell note to Fernandez. Raymond immediately invited her to New York, for fear of being exposed through publicity.

It wasn't long before Martha learned that Raymond was a swindler, but she decided to join him anyway, possibly because in her eyes he appeared to be her only hope for happiness. Martha however was too jealous to play the con game well, and the unholy alliance graduated to more serious activities. Together they ended up murdering three women and a child that Martha personally dispatched.

After being apprehended, Martha Beck and Raymond Fernandez were sent to Sing Sing prison in August, 1949, sentenced to die in the electric chair.

1949 – Raymond Fernandez and Mrs. Martha Beck

THE LONELY HEARTS KILLERS

NEW YORK, August 22, 1949 – Mrs. Martha Beck, convicted by a jury in the murder of Mrs. Janet Faye, was sentenced to die in the electric chair.

THE LONELY HEARTS KILLERS

NEW YORK – Police Emergency
Squad carries out the body
of Janet Faye.

OSSINING, NEW YORK, August 22,
1949 – Martha Beck enters what is
expected to be her last home, Sing
Sing Prison. Sentenced by Justice
Ferdinand Pecora to die in the
electric chair the week of October
10, Martha and her lover Raymond
Fernandez were rushed to the prison
in separate limousines.

JOHN GEORGE HAIGH "THE VAMPIRE KILLER"

John George Haigh was a notorious con man before he became a murderer. In February, 1949 he invited Mrs. Henrietta Helen Olivia Robarts Durand-Deacon to visit his "factory" at Crawley, in Sussex, so that they could better discuss Mrs. Durand-Deacon's idea for manufacturing false fingernails. The factory was nothing but an empty storeroom and when the lady arrived, Haigh promptly shot her. He then removed all her valuables and dumped the body into a vat containing sulfuric acid which had been readied for precisely that purpose. Haigh then drove back to his room at the Onslow Court Hotel in South Kensington.

A couple of days later, Haigh mentioned to another guest how worried he was about Mrs. Durand-Deacon, who was supposed to have met him days before, but hadn't shown up. The two went to the police and reported the woman's disappearance. The police, however, became suspicious of Haigh and, after discovering that his record was long and lurid, arrested him.

Believing the body to have been totally destroyed by the acid, Haigh admitted to murder, being certain the courts could not convict him without a corpse. He also confessed to six other similar slayings, telling police he was forced to kill to quench his thirst for human blood (a self-admitted ruse). Unfortunately for Haigh, parts of Mrs. Durand-Deacon and her effects were discovered, and he turned to a plea of insanity as his last hope. In listing his victims, Haigh threw in two young people from whom he could have had no financial gain, in an attempt to bolster the vampire theory.

The jury, however, took but fifteen minutes to decide that Haigh was very sane and very guilty of murder. He was hanged on August 10, 1949.

1949 – John George Haigh

"THE VAMPIRE KILLER"

HORSHAM, SUSSEX, ENGLAND, March 18, 1949 – Crowds gathered outside
the courthouse to watch arrivals for the Haigh murder trial; some queued
all night in order to gain admission to the trial. Three of the witnesses
shown arriving are, left to right: Mrs. E. Robbie, manageress of the Onslow
Court Hotel, Mrs. Kirkwood, and Mrs. C. Lane.

"THE VAMPIRE KILLER"

HORSHAM, SUSSEX, ENGLAND, March 18, 1949 – Handcuffed to a police officer, John George Haigh, 39-year-old company director, arrives at court for the prosecution's opening case against him for the murder of Mrs. Olivia Durand-Deacon.

OPPOSITE: **HORSHAM, SUSSEX, ENGLAND, March 5, 1949** – Suspected of murdering six persons and dissolving their bodies in a sulphuric acid bath, John George Haigh appears dapper and apparently untroubled. Police said he boasted that he sipped blood of his victims through a lemonade straw. In jail, he drinks tea whenever he can get it.

TOP: **CRAWLEY, SUSSEX, ENGLAND, 1949** – Dr. Keith Simpson, pathologist working with Scotland Yard, and his secretary, Jean Dunn, examine remains found in an abandoned factory here. As a result of the investigation, John George Haigh was arrested as the "vampire" slayer of six persons.

BOTTOM: **HORSHAM, SUSSEX, ENGLAND, March 14, 1949** – Crowds press around Haigh leaving courthouse. The alleged "vampire" killer was beseiged by girls and women who tried to get to him by breaking down the doors of a car which was transporting him between the courthouse and the prison. Haigh has also received a number of marriage proposals since the trial began.

"THE VAMPIRE KILLER"

HORSHAM, SUSSEX, ENGLAND, March 18, 1949 – Attorney General Sir Hartley Shawcross, K.C., leader of the prosecution, arrives at the Haigh murder trial.

LONDON, August 10, 1949 – Albert Pierrepont, the public executioner, as he arrives at Wandsworth Prison for the execution of John George Haigh

"THE VAMPIRE KILLER"

LONDON, August 10, 1949 – Crowds press outside the gates of Wandsworth
Prison to read the execution notice of John George Haigh, known as
"The Vampire Killer", who was hanged today.

THE BRINK'S ROBBERY

One of the most sophisticated robberies ever to be pulled off in the United States was that of the Brink's North Terminal Garage in Boston in 1950. For weeks before the robbery took place, thieves under the direction of Anthony Pino had surveyed the Brink's terminal. They walked about nights in their stocking feet measuring distances, locating doors, and determining the way in which they opened, all beneath the unsuspecting noses of the Brink's guards. One night they even removed locks from doors, fitted keys to them, and replaced the locks. Pino and his men went to the trouble of breaking into a burglar alarm company to better study the alarm system the Brink's people had installed.

The robbery itself was over in about twenty minutes and netted $1,218,211.

The thieves, wearing masks and crepe-soled shoes, relieved five very surprised and very embarrassed guards of the money.

The police and FBI agents were convinced they knew who had committed the crime but had no apparent way of proving their suspicions. Then they got lucky. One of the gang members, Joseph "Specs" O'Keefe, felt that he had not been given his rightful share of the take and wanted another $63,000. When the others refused, he turned informer and the thieves were arrested and subsequently sentenced for armed robbery.

BOSTON, January 21, 1950 – Velma Demaso stacks up a million dollars to give some idea of the amount of cash ($1,218,211) stolen from Brink's Armored Service by nine masked men. Incidently, the money is stacked deep inside the vault of one of Boston's leading banks.

THE BRINK'S ROBBERY

BOSTON, January 11, 1953 – Anthony Pino, 42, of Wollaston, Massachusetts, who has appeared as a witness before the grand jury investigating the million dollar Brink's robbery, is being held by immigration authorities for possible deportation. A native of Italy described as an ex-safe-cracker, Pino faces deportation under the newly enacted McCarran-Walter Bill.

TOP: **BOSTON, June 22, 1956** – Joseph "Specs" O'Keefe (center), who risked gangland vengeance to betray his confederates in the million dollar Brink's robbery, appears in Suffolk Superior Court today. O'Keefe, whose testimony helped put eight bandits behind bars for life, was freed under $5,000 bail after six years in jail. O'Keefe squealed on his pals because, he said, they bilked him out of his share of the Brink's loot.

BOTTOM: **BOSTON, August 6, 1956** – The eight suspects of the Brink's robbery appear in Boston's Suffolk Superior Court in a heavily guarded room as they wait for their trial to begin. A total of 169 indictments has been returned against the defendants.

Left to right: Michael Geagan, 47; James Faherty, 44; Thomas F. Richardson, 48; Joseph F. McGinnis, 52; Anthony Pino, 45; Vincent J. Costa, 41; Adolph "Jazz" Maffie, 44; and Henry Baker, 49.

WILLIE "THE ACTOR" SUTTON

Bankrobber Willie Sutton earned himself the nickname "The Actor" for his uncanny talent for disguise. He is estimated to have stolen more than one million dollars in his career which reached its heights in the 1940's and 1950's. Sutton was not only talented at disguising himself but also at escaping from prison. He was placed on the FBI "Ten Most Wanted" list in 1951. He was captured in 1952 and released from prison in 1969. His name once again became associated with that of a bank – this time he was doing television commercials for a bank.

In a strange twist, the man who had spotted Sutton in 1952 was murdered by Albert Anastasia's gunmen. Anastasia saw reports about Arnold Schuster, a law-abiding citizen who had turned Sutton in to the police as a public service. This "squealing" so angered Anastasia that he ordered the man killed. As far as is known, Sutton was in no way connected with the murder.

Once, when asked why he robbed banks, Sutton replied, "Because that's where the money is."

1952 – Willie Sutton

WILLIE "THE ACTOR" SUTTON

PHILADELPHIA, August 18, 1941 – Willie's sculpture is a "bust". Sergeant James J. Young examines a plaster head made by Willie Sutton for his artistic attempt at escape from the Eastern Penitentiary for the fourth time. Alert guards discovered the skillfully created mask of his face, which Sutton evidently intended to substitute for his own in the folds of his blanket to cover his escape for several hours. A rope braided from string was also found in his cell. The plan was discovered several weeks ago when he was seen making the mask from clay and plaster of paris stolen from a prison workshop. He was permitted to go on with his plans until the guards were ready to spring their own surprise. Sutton is serving a 25- to 50-year term.

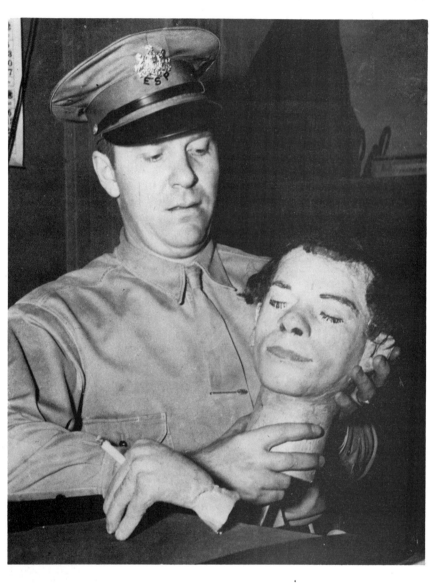

NEW BRITAIN, CONNECTICUT, October 22, 1970 – Willie "The Actor" Sutton has turned professional in his acting career, but is still in the banking business. The one-time nemesis of banks has been engaged by the New Britain Bank and Trust Company in Connecticut to promote their new photo credit card. "Now when I say I'm Willie Sutton, people believe me," he commented while shooting television commercials on location in Florida.

JOHN REGINALD CHRISTIE

John Reginald Halliday Christie was sexually abnormal. He seemed capable of the sexual act only when his partners were unconscious. In 1939 Christie killed Ruth Fuerst after either forcing or tricking her into inhaling gas and then raping her. He hid the body under the living room floor boards, out of sight of his wife, until he had time to bury it in the garden. Next came Muriel Eady, a friend of the Christies. Then came Mrs. Christie herself, except that she had not been raped. Apparently she and her husband had not been sexually active during their marriage, and she was not any more attractive when deceased. Mrs. Christie was murdered to gain Christie more freedom to pursue his nefarious activities.

Rita Nelson was murdered by Christie on January 2, 1953; Kathleen Maloney on January 12, 1953; and Hectorina McLennan on March 3, 1953.

Christie then vacated his London apartment which was subsequently rented to a Jamaican who discovered three of the bodies in a hidden cupboard and notified the police. The other three bodies were later discovered under the floor boards and in the garden. Christie was tried, convicted of murder, and executed on July 15, 1953.

John Reginald Christie, a mid-century "Bluebeard", convicted for the slaying of his wife and five other women

LONDON, 1953 – Derek Curtis-Bennett, Christie's solicitor, arrives at Old Bailey Court with his daughter at his side. He made a powerful plea for the "Strangler of Notting Hill", but the jury, ignoring pleas of insanity, decided Christie deserved to be executed.

LONDON, April 9, 1953 – Covering his face, John Reginald Christie, charged with the murder of his wife, Ethel, 54, arrives for an appearance at the West London Magistrates' Court. The 55-year-old haulage clerk is a suspect in the murders of five other women, whose bodies were found in the floors and walls of a slum apartment as well as in the garden.

DR. SAM SHEPPARD

According to the verdict of a Cleveland, Ohio jury, Dr. Sam Sheppard murdered his wife Marilyn on July 3, 1954, a fact Sheppard vehemently denied. Dr. Sam stated that on the morning of July 3 he went upstairs after being awakened by the screams of his wife and the sounds of a terrible fight. There he saw figures struggling with one another but was struck on the head and knocked unconscious before he could intervene. He regained enough consciousness to move out of the house, into the garden, and finally down to the beach, where he said he was again knocked unconscious. Sheppard later returned to the house and found his wife dead with thirty-three wounds on her body. The doctor had a hairline fracture of the vertebra and was taken to the hospital.

The police did not believe Sheppard's story and felt that he had even injured himself to make it look more realistic. They knew he had been having an affair with a lab technician and that he had talked of a divorce. The Cleveland jury on the Sheppard case believed the police version and Dr. Sam was sent to prison.

Sheppard was paroled in 1964 and in 1966 was acquitted of the murder charge in a retrial on the grounds that publicity had affected his first trial. Sheppard's second wife, Ariane, who had written faithfully to him in prison and married him immediately after his release in 1964, later divorced him saying that she sometimes feared for her life.

1954 – Dr. Sam Sheppard

DR. SAM SHEPPARD

CLEVELAND, OHIO, November 15, 1966 – Dr. Sam Sheppard (center) talks
with his lawyer F. Lee Bailey as Ariane Sheppard looks on. Bailey has
concluded his final arguments in the second murder trial of Sheppard
for the 1954 slaying of his first wife.

DR. SAM SHEPPARD

July 7, 1954 – Marilyn Sheppard, Dr. Sam Sheppard's first wife.

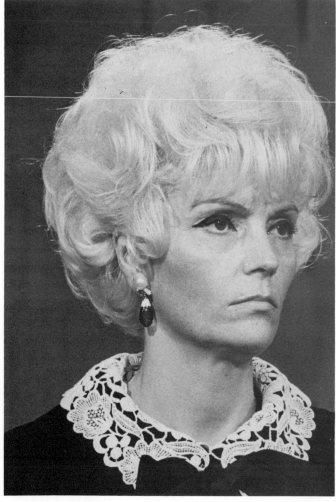

CLEVELAND, OHIO, December 19, 1968 – German-born Mrs. Ariane Sheppard faces newsmen to answer questions about her suit for divorce against Sheppard. Saying that she feared for her safety, she convinced the court to grant her an injunction restraining Sheppard from attempting any contact with her. Sheppard was convicted in the 1954 slaying of his first wife and acquitted in a retrial after serving nearly ten years in prison. The present Mrs. Sheppard married him three days after his release from jail. Their romance bloomed by mail while he was in prison and she was in Germany. In her divorce suit, Mrs. Sheppard charged gross neglect and extreme cruelty.

DR. SAM SHEPPARD

CLEVELAND, OHIO, December 21, 1954 – Framed by jail bars, Dr. Sam Sheppard shows the strain of awaiting word of his fate after the jury failed to reach a verdict. The jury began its fifth day of its record-breaking deliberation today.

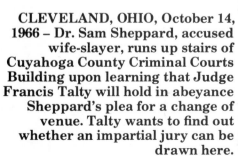

CLEVELAND, OHIO, October 14, 1966 – Dr. Sam Sheppard, accused wife-slayer, runs up stairs of Cuyahoga County Criminal Courts Building upon learning that Judge Francis Talty will hold in abeyance Sheppard's plea for a change of venue. Talty wants to find out whether an impartial jury can be drawn here.

"THE MAD BOMBER"

George Metesky, "The Mad Bomber", terrorized New York City from 1950 to 1957 by planting thirty-two live bombs in such places as Radio City Music Hall and Pennsylvania Railroad Station, injuring fifteen people and creating a seven-year period of municipal anxiety.

In an anonymous letter to a New York newspaper, the Mad Bomber stated that the Consolidated Edison Power Company had been responsible for his contracting tuberculosis. This started a massive search through the files of Con Ed, which ended with George Metesky emerging as the name of the man most likely to be the bomber. He was apprehended, found criminally insane and incarcerated in the New York State Mental Hospital from which he was later released.

WATERBURY, CONNECTICUT, January 18, 1975 – George Metesky, New York's "Mad Bomber", is shown (left) looking through bars of Manhattan Police Headquarters, January 22, 1957, and (right) as he left court, December 12, 1973, after charges against him were dismissed. Metesky now says that his biography is expected to be published in March and that a movie is to be made of his life. A bachelor, he is caring for his ailing sister, Mae, and has turned down a marriage proposal from a pen pal.

"THE MAD BOMBER"

NEW YORK, January 11, 1953 – A fireman from Engine Company No. 1, holds pieces of the homemade bomb which exploded in a Pennsylvania Station waiting room at the height of rush hour today. Police said no one was injured. Authorities said the bomb had been placed in a small baggage locker, and a passerby turned in a fire alarm following the explosion. The blast caused no panic among thousands of commuters.

BROOKLYN, NEW YORK, February 19, 1957 – Still flashing his characteristic broad grin, George Metesky, the 53-year-old "Mad Bomber", peers out from behind bars before his arraignment in Kings County Court for the bombing December 2, 1956, of the Brooklyn Paramount Theater, where seven persons were injured. The arraignment made the Waterbury, Connecticut toolmaker liable to an added 235 years in prison on seven counts of attempted murder and assorted other charges. Metesky has been undergoing psychiatric examinations at Bellevue Hospital. He is already faced with more than 1,000 years in jail if found sane and guilty of Manhattan bombings attributed to him.

THE PROFUMO SCANDAL

In early 1963 Prime Minister Harold Macmillan's government was rocked by one of those sex scandals Britons seem indignantly attached to. It had been discovered that London society osteopath Stephen Ward was moonlighting as a procurer and organizer of sex parties. He introduced his girls, two of whom were Mandy Rice-Davis and Christine Keeler, to London's most influential men.

Unfortunately for the Macmillan Government, War Minister John Profumo was one of those men. Profumo might not have been forced to resign, but he made an error in denying the entire affair. It was also learned that Miss Keeler had been having sexual relations with a Soviet military attaché, Captain Ivanov, at the same time as she had been seeing Profumo. The opposition and the public wondered whether or not Profumo was a security risk, and Macmillan decided to remove him fom office.

Profumo returned to private life and eventually became rehabilitated. Ward went on trial for living on earnings obtained in an immoral manner. Completely discredited and deserted by the now scandal-conscious friends he once had in society, Ward committed suicide.

LONDON, February 24, 1959 – John Profumo, Joint Parliamentary Undersecretary of State for Foreign Affairs (left) with his actress wife, Valerie Hobson, at a military attachés' reception held in the Soviet Embassy. With them are left to right: Major General Efimov, Soviet Army Attaché; Mrs. Efimov; and Colonel Konstantinov, Soviet Air Attaché.

THE PROFUMO SCANDAL

LONDON, June 7, 1963 – Red-headed model Christine Keeler, 21, leaves for the final day of trial of West Indian singer James Aloysius "Lucky" Gordon, who was charged with beating her. Gordon, who accused Miss Keeler of being a call girl, was sentenced to three years in prison for assault, but was acquitted of wounding her with intent to do bodily harm. The Labor Party pressed the Government to determine whether security had been endangered by resigned War Minister John Profumo's relations with Miss Keeler, who also dated Eugene Ivanov, former Assistant Naval Attaché at the Soviet Embassy.

THE PROFUMO SCANDAL

LONDON, July 1, 1963 – Clutching a stuffed toy lion, Marilyn "Mandy" Rice-Davis smiles charmingly for photographers at London Airport before a holiday flight to Majorca, Spain. "Mandy", friend of Christine Keeler who was partly responsible for the downfall of former British War Minister John Profumo, testified at the Parliamentary inquiry into the activities of society portraitist and osteopath, Dr. Stephen Ward. In reply to an American tourist's query, "Who is this nice young lady?" Miss Rice-Davis said, "I'm notorious."

THE PROFUMO SCANDAL

LONDON, June 11, 1963 – Captain Eugene Ivanov and his wife at an embassy reception in 1961. Ivanov is the former Assistant Naval Attaché of the Soviet Embassy who shared the favors of London playgirl Christine Keeler with British ex-War Minister John Profumo. Ivanov, reportedly described by Miss Keeler as a "wonderful huggy bear of a man," was recalled to Moscow in December, 1962, long before the scandal that threatened the Conservative Government of Prime Minister Harold Macmillan came to light.

LONDON, July 25, 1963 – A London bobby wipes from his uniform the spattered remains of an egg hurled by someone outside the Old Bailey as Christine Keeler left after giving evidence in the trial of Dr. Stephen Ward.

THE PROFUMO SCANDAL

LONDON, July 29, 1963 – Dr. Stephen Ward smiles as he leaves Old Bailey after the sixth day of his trial on morals charges. Dr. Ward's defense abruptly rested its case in the vice trial with a plea to jurors not to sacrifice Ward to the public demand for punishment of those respon - sible for Britain's sex and security scandal.

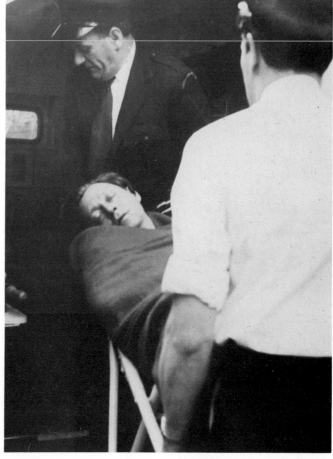

LONDON, August 2, 1963 – Dr. Stephen Ward is carried to a waiting ambulance from the Chelsea apartment where he was found unconscious early July 31, after an apparent overdose of barbituates. A criminal court jury found Ward guilty on two charges of living off earnings from prostitution. Julia Gulliver, 22, Ward's latest girl friend, said that if Ward dies, she will expose a "whole crowd" of upper crust friends who failed to testify at his vice trial.

THE PROFUMO SCANDAL

LONDON, November 18, 1971 – Queen Elizabeth shakes hands with her former War Minister John Profumo as she opens a social welfare center. It was their first meeting in eight years. Profumo met the Queen as a trustee of the Atlee Foundation which operates the center

LONDON, June 16, 1975 – John Profumo (right), who was made a C.B.E. (Commander of the British Empire) for his work amongst London's poor in the Queen's Birthday Honours List, laughs as he gets congratulations from barrow boys in a street market near his offices in London's East End. Profumo, who resigned as Conservative Government War Minister in the 1963 scandal, has worked at Toynbee Hall for the last eleven years as a volunteer worker helping East Enders fight poverty.

THE GREAT TRAIN ROBBERY

On August 8, 1963 the mail train from Glasgow to London was stopped near Cheddington Station and robbed of over 2,500,000 pounds sterling. The robbery had been planned for months and had obviously been carried out with great precision. The story began some eight months before when the delivery of some 62,500 pounds to a bank at London Airport was stolen. The money had been taken to cover plans and hire men for the big job – the mail train.

What led to the downfall of a number of the robbers was their carelessness in not eradicating fingerprints at their hideout, Leathersdale Farm. The men were under the impression that some member of the gang would follow along and remove any fingerprints after they had left, but this just never happened. When some people around the farm grew suspicious, the police moved in and found both the telltale prints and empty mailbags.

All members of the gang were eventually captured but two have since made successful prison escapes and are still at large. It is probable that the sentencing of the mail robbers created more of a stir than their actual crime. Most of the men were given prison terms of thirty years, and that for a crime in which only one man, the train engineer, was injured.

MONTREAL, January 26, 1968 – This photo of Charles Frederick Wilson was taken by the Montreal Police after he was arrested at his home, living under the alias of Ronald Alloway and sporting a beard. He will be deported to England to serve the rest of his thirty-year sentence for his part in the Great Train Robbery in 1963.

TOP: **CHEDDINGTON, ENGLAND, August 8, 1963** – Broken glass litters the floor of one of the Royal Mail coaches that were ransacked early today when a thirty-man gang robbed the Glasgow-to-London Aberdeen Express. A post office spokesman said the gang made off with more than 2,500,000 pounds, making this the biggest rail robbery in British history.

BOTTOM: **OAKLEY, ENGLAND, August 13, 1963** – The abandoned Leatherslade farmhouse after discovery by Scotland Yard that it had been used as a base by the bandits who got away with several million dollars in Britain's Great Train Robbery, August 8. Detectives found empty mailbags scattered around, but no cash and no bandits.

THE GREAT TRAIN ROBBERY

OAKLEY, ENGLAND, August 13, 1963 – Gerald MacArthur (right), Scotland
Yard's superindendent of detectives, speaks with reporters after the
abandoned farmhouse was discovered. MacArthur said the bandits had
spent about three weeks there, before and after the August 8 robbery. An
old World War II airstrip near the house led detectives to believe the gang
may have loaded the loot aboard a plane after they counted it and
fled to the continent.

THE GREAT TRAIN ROBBERY

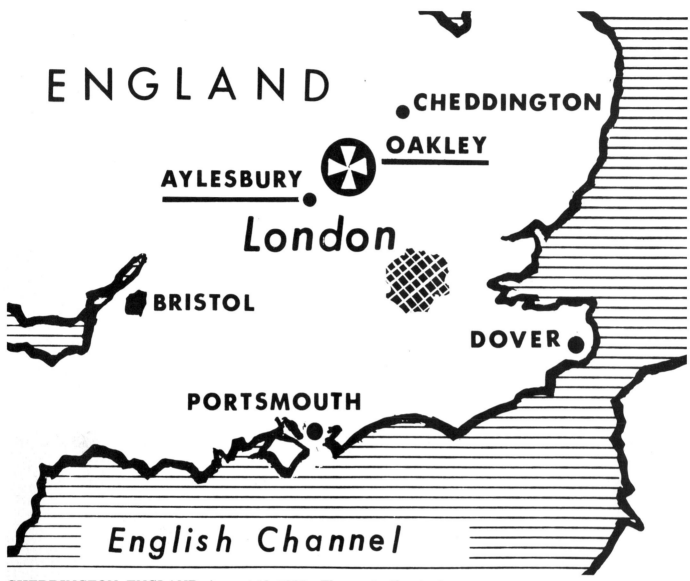

CHEDDINGTON, ENGLAND, August 13, 1963 – The post office train was stopped about two miles north of here by signals apparently set by the gang. The fireman and engineer were thrown off the train while the gang uncoupled the engine and two sealed mail cars from the rest of the train and drove another mile down the rails to where they then ransacked the cars. Some forty postal employees on the rest of the train were unaware of the robbery until it was over.

The bandits split up their loot in an abandoned farmhouse at Oakley (Maltese cross), where empty mail bags were found. A Scotland Yard spokesman said the "house was well stocked with food," and that it appeared the bandits had "left in rather a hurry." Oakley is two miles from where the signal lights were crossed to stop the train.

TOP: **LONDON, August 22, 1963 –** Their work appeared to be coming to an end today as Scotland Yard distributed these three pictures of men wanted in connection with the Great Train Robbery. Left to right: James E. White, 45, cafe proprietor; Charles Frederick Wilson, 31, called a bookie; and Bruce Richard Reynolds, 41, car and antique dealer.

BOTTOM: **LONDON, August 30, 1963 –** Scotland Yard officials released this photo in connection with the August 8 train robbery. Left to right: Bruce Richard Reynolds; his wife, Mrs. Frances Reynolds; Mrs. Barbara Maria Daly; and her husband, John Thomas Daly. Police believe Reynolds and Daly will be able to help in inquiries about the holdup.

THE GREAT TRAIN ROBBERY

LINSLADE, ENGLAND, November 9, 1968 – Bruce Richard Reynolds, the last of England's Great Train Robbery bandits, looks about him as he arrives at court. He was captured yesterday at a seaside hideout, where he had been living with his wife and six-year-old son. Reynolds, 37, is one of twelve men accused of the 1963 Royal Mail Train robbery.

BOURNEMOUTH, ENGLAND, August 15, 1963 – Detective-Sergeant Stan Davies, 44 (left), and Detective-Constable Charles Case, 29, smile broadly after they arrested two men in connection with the Great Train Robbery. The men were trying to garage two cars in which detectives found $280,000.

THE GREAT TRAIN ROBBERY

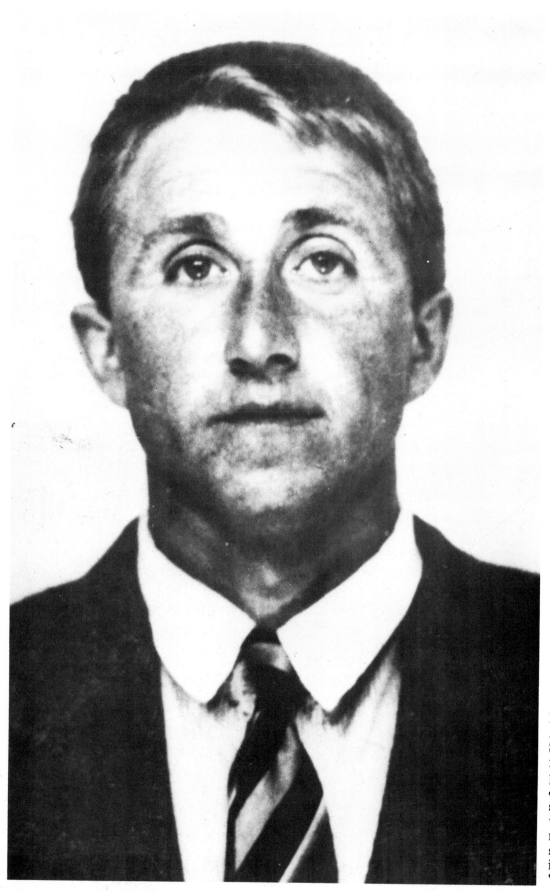

LONDON, August 23, 1963 – Scotland Yard released this photograph of Roy John James, 28, sought in connection with the mail train robbery. James is a silversmith, known in the underworld as "The Weasel".

THE JOHN F. KENNEDY ASSASSINATION

On November 22, 1963 in Dallas, Texas at approximately 12:30 P.M., President John F. Kennedy was shot to death apparently with a mail-order rifle fired by Lee Harvey Oswald. Oswald, an employee of the Texas School Book Depository, had learned from a local newspaper that the President's motorcade would pass beneath the windows of the building in which he worked. On the morning of November 22, Oswald took up his vigil by a sixth floor window in the Book Depository. When the motorcade passed he shot three times, killing Kennedy and seriously wounding then Texas Governor John Connally.

Oswald then hid his rifle among some crates in the depository and strolled leisurely from the building, stopping first in the canteen for a cold drink. He made his way home where he picked up a pistol. After leaving his home Oswald was stopped and interrogated by Dallas Police Officer J. D. Tippit whom he shot. He fled and some hours later was apprehended in a Dallas movie theater. Two days later, Oswald was dead, having been shot by Jack Ruby while in custody in the Dallas jail.

After exhaustive investigations the Warren Commission came to the conclusion that Lee Harvey Oswald had murdered President Kennedy on his own for obscure political reasons. Many people believed and still do believe otherwise, but the only real evidence available points to the fact that President Kennedy was murdered for unknown reasons by this political malcontent. The case seems destined to be reopened and the possibility of a conspiracy reexamined.

DALLAS, November 22, 1963 – President John F. Kennedy slumps into the arms of his wife immediately after a sniper's bullet slammed into his head while he was riding in a motorcade here. The photograph was taken with a Polaroid camera by a woman watching the motorcade.

THE JOHN F. KENNEDY ASSASSINATION

THE JOHN F. KENNEDY ASSASSINATION

DALLAS, December 22, 1963 – The County Courthouse will be the scene of a defense-requested hearing on a writ of habeas corpus to determine whether Jack Ruby will be freed on bail. Ruby will go on trial February 23, 1964 for the November 24, 1963 shooting of Lee Harvey Oswald. The diagramed photograph shows places significant in the case: spot where President Kennedy was shot (Maltese cross); sniper's perch in Texas School Book Depository Building.

OPPOSITE PAGE: **This photograph (Warren Commission exhibit No. 134) shows Lee Harvey Oswald holding a rifle and carrying a revolver at his hip. This same rifle was found on the sixth floor of the Texas School Book Depository Building, November 22, 1963.**

THE JOHN F. KENNEDY ASSASSINATION

ANDREWS AIRFORCE BASE, MARYLAND, November 22, 1963 –
Mrs. Jacqueline Kennedy, her clothing spattered with the blood of her
assassinated husband, watches as the body of the dead President is placed
in an ambulance. Mrs. Kennedy and Attorney General Robert F. Kennedy
(partially hidden) rode in the ambulance to Bethesda Naval Hospital.

DALLAS, November 24, 1963 – Even as America buried its fallen President, Americans saw before their eyes on television Jack Ruby lunge through a crowd of police and news reporters and shoot down Lee Harvey Oswald, as shown in this sequence.

TOP: **LONDON, November 22, 1963** – The world learns of President Kennedy's death.

BOTTOM: **WASHINGTON, D.C., November 23, 1963** – President Lyndon B. Johnson, in a rain-splattered car, leaves his home for his office in the Executive Office Building. The successor to the slain President Kennedy wears the anxieties of the tragic hours that have elapsed since the assassination, November 22.

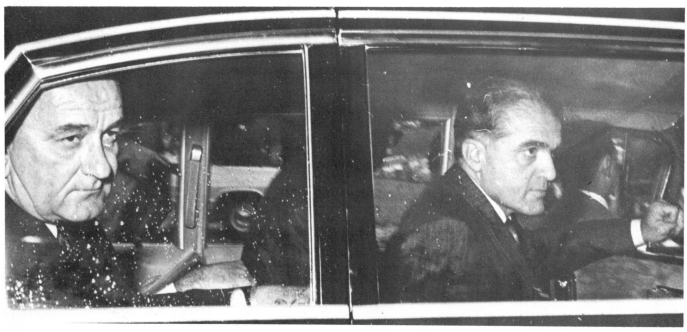

THE BOSTON STRANGLER

For nearly three years beginning in 1963, the city of Boston and its outlying suburbs were to live in the stranglehold of fear brought on by a series of bizarre murders, which left, all told, thirteen women dead – without a single clue as to the killer. As one after another of the bodies were found strangled and sexually molested, the name "the Boston Strangler" came to be as much a household word as Jack the Ripper. Women in Boston, not knowing whom or where the Boston Strangler would strike next and paralyzed with fear, refused to open their doors to unfamiliar voices and would only venture into the streets if escorted.

These killings became one of the most stunning multiple murders in recorded history, involving one of the most persistent manhunts ever mounted in Massachusetts, and yet to this day no man has actually stood trial for these crimes as the Boston Strangler. Who was this killer who was responsible for the known deaths of thirteen women and for the terror that gripped a city?

Who defied apprehension despite the exhaustive efforts of state and local police departmens and the FBI?

It turned out that the police had him in custody all the time. Albert H. DeSalvo, a 34-year-old mental patient already known to police for a long history of sexually perverse crimes, confessed in 1966 to being the Boston Strangler. He was able to describe verifiable details of the crimes that only the killer could have known. Yet he was found medically ill and legally insane and thereby unable to stand trial. His attorney, F. Lee Bailey, convinced that DeSalvo was indeed the Strangler, encouraged the presiding judge to have DeSalvo committed to the Bridgewater State Mental Hospital for life. Five weeks after being put in the hospital he escaped, but was recaptured thirty hours later and returned to his prison ward.

NEW YORK, February 25, 1967 – F. Lee Bailey, defense attorney for confessed Boston Strangler Albert DeSalvo, looks at a UPI telephoto of DeSalvo who was captured thirty hours after escaping from a state mental hospital.

THE BOSTON STRANGLER

CAMBRIDGE, MASSACHUSETTS, January 10, 1967 – Albert DeSalvo, 35, is escorted into Cambridge Superior Court, where, in a preliminary preceding of his scheduled trial on sex, assault and burglary charges, a psychiatrist testified that DeSalvo is "medically and legally insane."

THE BOSTON STRANGLER

BOSTON, January 6, 1954 – Photographs of eight women who have been strangled to death in the Boston area recently. Left to right, top row: Rachel Lazarus; Helen E. Blake; Ida Irga; Mrs. J. Delaney. Bottom row: Patricia Bissette; Daniela M. Saunders; Mary A. Sullivan; Mrs. Israel Goldberg.

RICHARD SPECK

Richard Speck had very little formal education and earned his money as a seaman when not drunk or under the influence of drugs. August 13, 1966 found him, by chance, in front of 2319 E. 100th Street on Chicago's South Side, drunk and high on barbituates. He forced entry into the apartment occupied by nine student nurses with a knife and pistol, and proceeded to bind the six nurses present. He then waited for the others to return home and bound them too.

After securing their money, Speck led the girls one by one from the room where they were tied up, and stabbed or strangled them. He sexually assaulted his eighth victim before murdering her. One of the nurses, Corazon Amurao, amazingly managed to hide under a bed and was overlooked by Speck. After he left, she ran screaming from the apartment and was able to give the police a description of the killer.

After a number of days, Speck attempted to slit his wrists and was identified as the mass murderer when brought to the hospital. Speck was convicted of murder and sentenced to death. The Supreme Court soon after struck down capital punishment, and Speck's death sentence was changed to several consecutive life terms, totaling more than four hundred years.

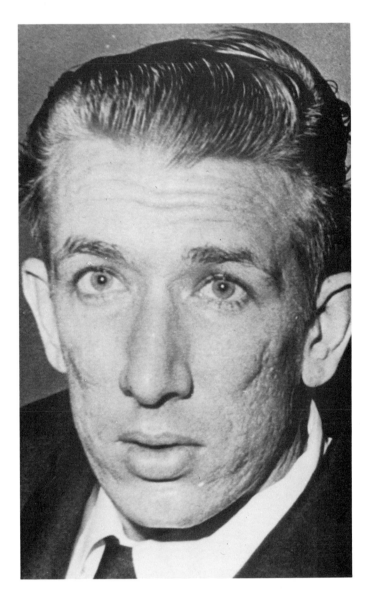

CHICAGO, August 18, 1966 – Richard Speck, 24, accused slayer of eight nurses, calmly stares into the camera while in court. His lawyer, Gerald Getty, challenged the prosecution to join him in appointing a blue ribbon panel of psychiatrists to determine whether Speck is sane.

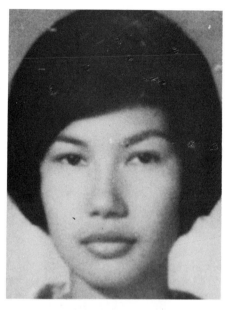

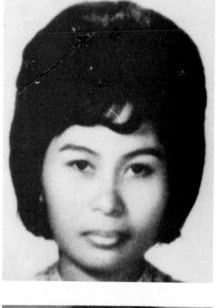

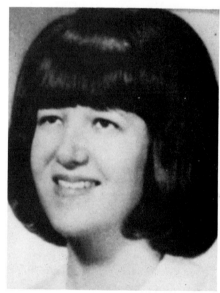

CHICAGO, July 14, 1966 – The eight student nurses found slain in the duplex living quarters of the South Chicago Community Hospital early today. The nude bodies were found stabbed and strangled. Left to right, top row: Mary A. Jordan; Marlita Gargullo; Valentina Passion. Middle row: Pamela Wilkening; Gloria Davy; Nina Schmale. Bottom row: Patricia Matuse; Susan Farris.

RICHARD SPECK

CHICAGO, July 18, 1966 – Above and below: two of the bloodstained bedrooms where the bodies of eight student nurses were found stabbed or strangled. One of the nurses escaped by rolling under a bed after being tied up.

RICHARD SPECK

PEORIA, ILLINOIS, April 17, 1967 –
Convicted slayer Richard Speck is
escorted by shotgun-wielding policemen from the Peoria County Courthouse as he is transferred to Chicago.
He was found guilty of the murder
of eight Chicago student
nurses last July.

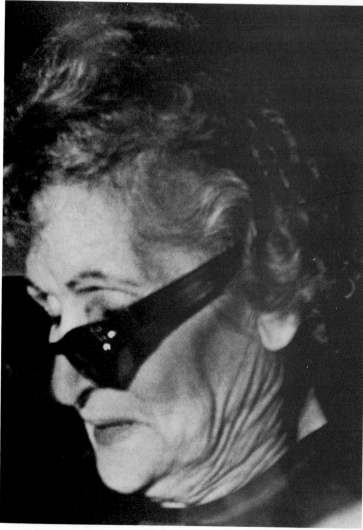

PEORIA, ILLINOIS, April 12, 1967 –
The mother of Richard Speck, Mrs.
Margret Lindbergh of Dallas, Texas,
ducks into a car to evade photographers after testifying today about
when her son left for Chicago. As
Mrs. Lindbergh left the court, she
gestured to her son.

RICHARD SPECK

CHICAGO, July 17, 1966 – George Gregrich relaxes in his 90-cents-a-day room in a skidrow hotel while he tells how he heard a thump on his door and, going to answer it, found a stranger covered with blood. Gregrich helped the man to his bed and persuaded the hotel clerk to call the police. The stranger has been identified as Richard Speck, prime suspect in the murder of eight student nurses. Speck was treated for slashes on his arm and wrist in an apparent suicide attempt.

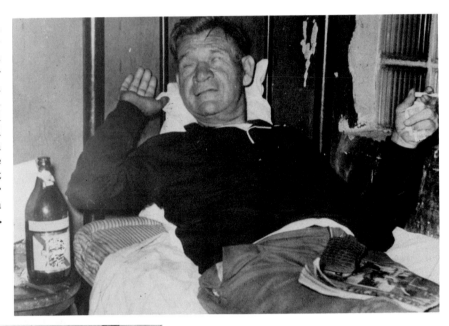

CHICAGO, July 20, 1966 – The blood spattered hotel room in which Speck was found after an apparent suicide attempt.

CHARLES WHITMAN

Ex-marine Charles Whitman's troubles apparently began in March of 1966 when his mother decided to leave his father at whose hands she had suffered repeated beatings. The incident somehow unleashed a homicidal fury in Whitman, which was to culminate in the killing of eighteen people including his mother and wife.

Whitman felt that his visits to the psychiatrist were not helping and decided to end his own life along with the lives of many others. He murdered his mother on July 31, 1966 to put her out of her supposed misery; he then murdered his wife, Kathy, to spare her the embarrassment of his actions.

After these killings, Whitman packed a trunk with weapons, ammunition and food and set off for the University of Texas Tower where he shot and killed the receptionist and two visitors. He then proceeded to the top of the tower and picked off thirteen other innocent people whose lives he apparently felt were no more worth living than his own.

Finally, Austin, Texas patrolman Ramiro Martinez led an assault on Whitman's position which ended in the patrolman's injury and the sniper's death. In all, eighteen people had been killed and thirty wounded.

LAKE WORTH, FLORIDA, August 3, 1966 – These photos were released by the father of Charles Whitman, the University of Texas sniper who killed fifteen persons including his wife and mother. Left: Charles at age 2½. Right: 13-year-old Charles with younger brothers Patrick and John (front).

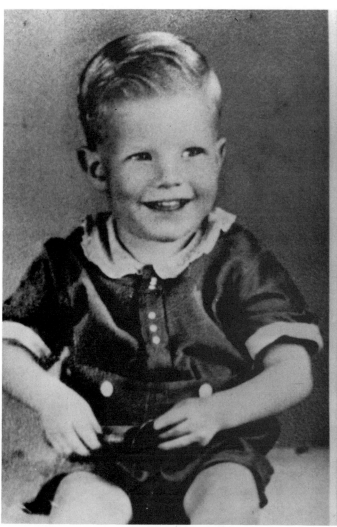

CHARLES WHITMAN

AUSTIN, TEXAS, August 2, 1966 – Charles Whitman is shown here sleeping on a couch with a dog at his feet and a book he apparently was reading leaning against him. This was one of the pictures on the film left by Whitman who was killed during his sniper spree August 1.

AUSTIN, TEXAS, August 1, 1966 – Charles Whitman, 24, whom police identified as the sniper who staged a wild noontime attack on people from the University of Texas Tower. A non-resident student from Florida, he carried nineteen hours this spring with a B average and was registered for an unusually heavy load of fourteen hours for the shorter summer semester.

UNIVERSITY OF TEXAS

TOP: **AUSTIN, TEXAS, August 2, 1966** – Diagram view of the University of Texas campus shows where victims fell during Whitman's sniper rampage. Numbers by each figure indicate the number of dead or wounded found at each location. (Diagram does not show all victims found.) Whitman killed eighteen and wounded at least thirty persons on the campus, before he was killed by police.

BOTTOM: **AUSTIN, TEXAS, August 1, 1966** – An unidentified girl hides behind a statue as a man lies wounded on the ground (left) during the sniper fire.

CHARLES WHITMAN

AUSTIN, TEXAS, August 1, 1966 – Police bullets kick up dust (arrow) around the University of Texas Tower clock as police return the sniper fire. After an eighty-minute reign of terror, sniper Charles Whitman was shot and killed.

AUSTIN, TEXAS, August 1, 1966 – Charles Whitman's arsenal, found by police on the observation platform of the University of Texas Tower.

CHARLES WHITMAN

AUSTIN, TEXAS, August 1, 1966 – Patrolman Ramiro Martinez is led from the scene after he shot and killed sniper Charles Whitman. Martinez inched his way around a wall at the top of the twenty-seven story University of Texas Tower and fired six bullets into Whitman with his service revolver after the sniper shot at him.

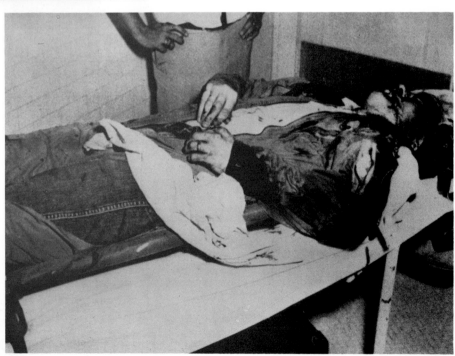

AUSTIN, TEXAS, August 1, 1966 – Charles Whitman's body lies on a stretcher after he was killed by police.

THE MARTIN LUTHER KING ASSASSINATION

On the evening of April 4, 1968, Dr. Martin Luther King, Jr. lay bleeding, an hour away from death, on the balcony of his motel room in Memphis, Tennessee. King had been shot by a petty criminal, a man who for all outward intents and purposes had no reason to shoot the civil rights leader. James Earl Ray had served time in Florida, Illinois and Missouri, and each crime had involved money, never politics.

After the shooting, Ray escaped to England by way of Canada on a Canadian passport. He moved from hotel to hotel while in London, took an unexplained side trip to Lisbon, returned to London and was about to fly to Brussels when he was apprehended at Heathrow Airport. The assassin was extradited to the United States and pleaded guilty to the crime of murder. He was sentenced to 99 years in prison.

Some months later, Ray changed his plea and sought a new trial. Whether or not Ray was working at the behest of others in the assassination is still undetermined, but the investigation will be continued.

July 1, 1964 – Martin Luther King, Jr.

MARTIN LUTHER KING ASSASSINATION

ATLANTA, GEORGIA, April 27, 1960 – Integration leader Reverend Martin Luther King, Jr. pulls up the four-foot cross that was burned on the front lawn of his home last night. With King is his son, Martin Luther III, aged 2. The cross, symbol of the Ku Klux Klan, was among many that were burned at a number of dwellings of blacks throughout the city.

MEMPHIS, TENNESSEE, April 8, 1968 – A view through a simulated telescopic gunsight made from the flophouse bathroom window sill showing the scene the sniper saw as he squeezed off the shot that killed Dr. King. The balcony of the Lorraine Motel where King and his friends were talking can be seen in the upper left quadrant, to the left of the door with the wreath.

MEMPHIS, TENNESSEE, April 5, 1968 – This is the view from Room 306 of the Lorraine Motel, occupied by Dr. King, looking toward the building from which the sniper's shot was said to have been fired. The shot is believed to have been from the fourth window from the right side of the building.

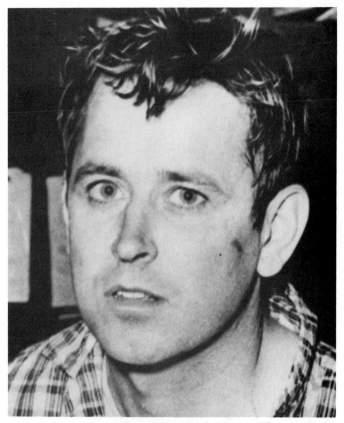

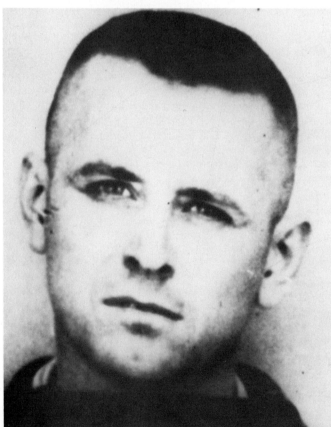

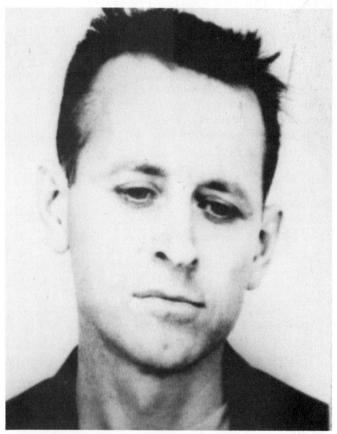

WASHINGTON, D.C., April 20, 1968 – James Earl Ray, 40, being sought in connection with the slaying of Dr. Martin Luther King, was placed on the FBI list of "Ten Most Wanted" fugitives today. Also sought under the alias of Eric Starvo Galt, Ray escaped from Missouri State Prison April 23, 1967. With a criminal record dating back to 1949, Ray is pictured in these photos from various prisons. Left to right, top: 1952, Joliet; 1959, Miami. Bottom: 1960 and 1966, Jefferson City, Missouri.

OVERLEAF: **Dr. Martin Luther King, Jr., in a moment of reflection**

THE ROBERT F. KENNEDY ASSASSINATION

Senator Robert F. Kennedy had just won the California State presidential primary and had thanked his supporters at a victory rally. His informal remarks were full of justifiable pride and he indicated his optimism about the upcoming Illinois primary. A few minutes later as Kennedy was walking toward a rear exit of the Ambassador Hotel, Sirhan Bishara Sirhan removed a pistol from behind a Kennedy campaign poster he had been carrying and shot the Senator in the head. Kennedy died twenty-five hours later.

Sirhan, a Palestinian, was proud of himself. He joked with the officers who guarded him, having them taste his coffee to make sure there was no poison in it. At one point he told an officer he couldn't understand what drove the so-called Boston Strangler to murder all those women.

Sirhan Sirhan was tried and convicted of the murder of Robert Kennedy. He was sentenced to die in the gas chamber but was spared execution when the Supreme Court ruled that capital punishment was unconstitutional.

The California courts have just recently reopened the Robert Kennedy Assassination Case to determine whether Sirhan acted alone or in consort with others.

1969 – Sirhan Bishara Sirhan

THE ROBERT KENNEDY ASSASSINATION

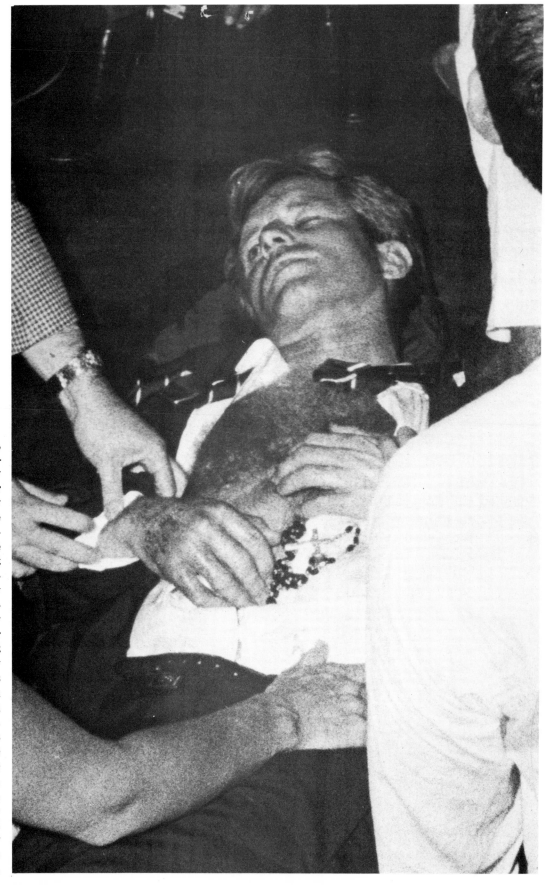

LOS ANGELES, June 5, 1968 – Clutching his rosary beads, Senator Robert F. Kennedy lies wounded on the floor of the Ambassador Hotel after he was shot last night by an assailant following his victory speech in the California primary election. The brother of the late President John F. Kennedy died early this morning after a team of surgeons tried in vain to save his life. Murder charges were expected to be filed against the accused gunman, Sirhan Sirhan, 24, the Jordanian immigrant seized moments after Kennedy fell with a bullet in his brain.

THE ROBERT KENNEDY ASSASSINATION

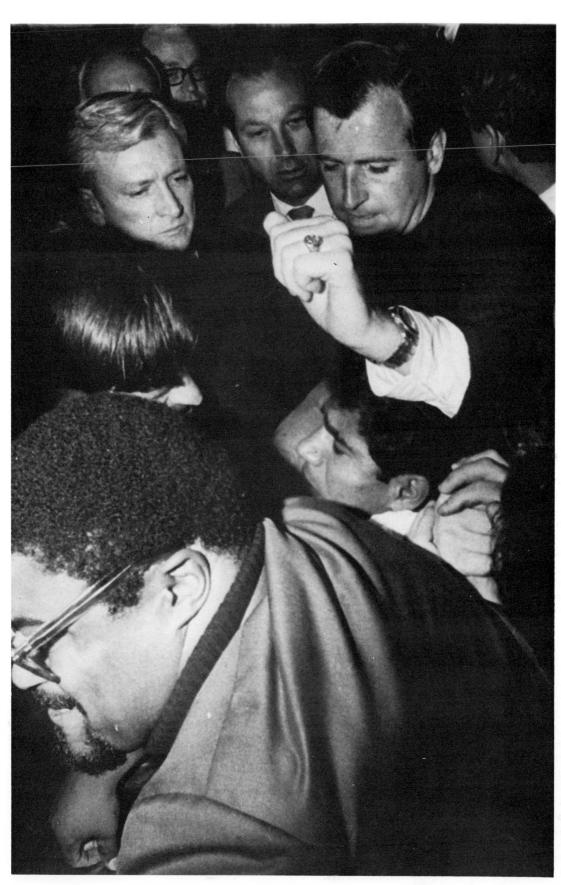

LOS ANGELES, June 5, 1968 – A member of the Kennedy party, ex-football star Roosevelt Grier, is shown pulling Sirhan from the crowd immediately after the shooting.

THE ROBERT KENNEDY ASSASSINATION

LOS ANGELES, June 5, 1968 – Sweat-shirted suspect, Sirhan Sirhan, is taken from the Ambassador Hotel.

THE ROBERT KENNEDY ASSASSINATION

AMMAN, JORDAN, June 19, 1968 – Bishara Sirhan studies a Jordanian magazine which bears a picture of his son, Sirhan Bishara Sirhan, 24. The father was in Amman to draw money from a bank for a trip to the United States.

BEIRUT, LEBANON, April 16, 1969 – This is one of the posters depicting Sirhan Sirhan as a heroic guerrilla, which appeared on the streets of Arab capitals in the Middle East. The poster carried a picture of the Palestine-born Sirhan and the words, "Sirhan Bishara Sirhan, a commando not an assassin." Commando sources said the posters were designed to press the view that Sirhan, in shooting Senator Robert Kennedy, was acting on behalf of all dispossessed Palestinians in a move aimed at Israel, which Kennedy supported.

CHARLES MANSON

In August, 1969 Charles "Tex" Watson, Susan Atkins, Patricia Krenwinkel, and Leslie Van Houten murdered actress Sharon Tate, eight months pregnant, and four others at the estate Miss Tate shared with her husband Roman Polanski. Two days later the same group broke into the home of Leno and Rosemary La Bianca, killed them and scrawled messages on the walls with the blood of their victims.

The four murderers were soon discovered to belong to a "family" headed by Charles Manson. Manson, 34, had been in and out of prisons and reform schools for almost twenty years. He was the self-appointed leader of the family which seemed to practice a mixture of free love, experimental drug highs, and guerrilla tactics, with Manson acting as a Christ figure.

Manson, who supposedly masterminded the murders, and the girls were brought to trial and convicted of murder in January, 1971. Manson laughed and joked throughout the trial and seemed to revel in the attention he was getting. All four ("Tex" Watson was tried and convicted separately) were sentenced to die in the gas chamber. The Supreme Court's capital punishment ruling voided that decision, and they were all given life imprisonment. In 1978 they will all be eligible to apply for parole.

On September 5, 1975 the family was heard from again when Lynette "Squeaky" Fromme, the acting family head while Manson is in jail, was arrested for attempting to assassinate President Gerald Ford in Sacramento, California as he walked from his hotel to the California State House to deliver a speech on violent crime in America. The attempt was foiled by Secret Service agents.

1969 – Charles Manson

CHARLES MANSON

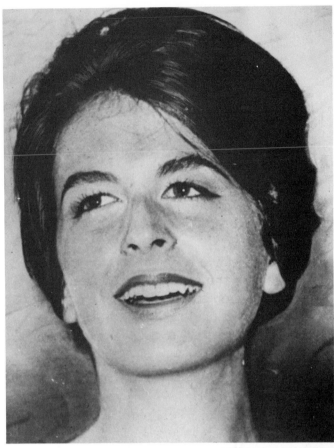

TOP LEFT: **LOS ANGELES, August 13, 1969 – Shown in a 1965 photograph, actress Sharon Tate was one of the victims of the grisly stabbing and shooting deaths on August 9.**

TOP RIGHT: **LOS ANGELES, August 9, 1969 – Abigail Folger, heiress to the Folger coffee fortune, has been identified as one of the five victims in the Tate murders.**

BOTTOM LEFT: **LOS ANGELES, August 9, 1969 – One of the five Tate murder victims, Voyteck Frykowski was a Polish writer and producer, living with Abigail Folger. The two other victims were men's hairstylist Jay Sebring and 18-year-old Steven Earl Parent.**

LOS ANGELES, March 19, 1970 – The three female suspects in the Tate murder case sing as they march to court for a hearing. Dressed for the occasion, their party dresses are in direct contrast to the "hippie" attire dress code of the Manson Family as well as the prison garb they were later to wear throughout their trial. Left to right: Susan Atkins, Patricia Krenwinkel, and Leslie Van Houten.

LOS ANGELES, August 5, 1970 – Hamming it up for photographers through the window of the Sheriff's van are Patricia Krenwinkle (left), Leslie Van Houten, and Susan Atkins (right).

LOS ANGELES, March 29, 1971 – Hair shorn and bearing "X" symbols scratched into their foreheads, Susan Atkins (left), Patricia Krenwinkel and Leslie Van Houten (right) make a seemingly cheerful trio as they are led to the courtroom where a jury decreed death in the gas chamber for them and Manson.

CHARLES MANSON

LOS ANGELES, March 5, 1970 – Susan Denise Atkins peers from behind iron bars at the men's section of Central Jail after she conferred with Charles Manson. (The prosecution hoped for a time that Susan would turn State's Witness, but Manson evidently convinced her to maintain a united defense.)

LOS ANGELES, August 20, 1970 – State's star witness, Linda Kasabian, 21, was along with defendants on the nights of the Tate and LaBianca murders, though she did not take part in any of the violence. A member of the Manson Family for only a short time, she was evidently taken along because she had a valid drivers' license. Granted immunity for her part in testifying for the State, Linda told newsmen that she intended to "go to the wilderness" with her children and continue to lead the life of a hippie.

CHARLES MANSON

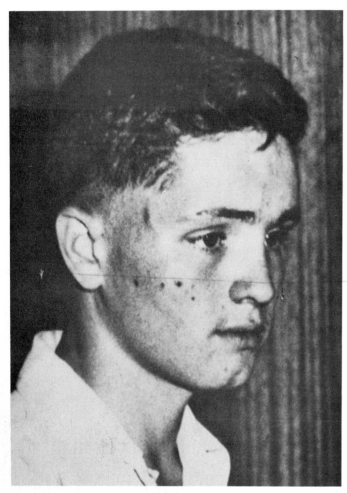

INDIANAPOLIS, INDIANA, December 19, 1969 – Charles Manson, now 34, is shown at the age of 14 when he lived in Indianapolis after having been released from a juvenile home. His mother had abandoned him, and he had become a ward of the court.

PHILADELPHIA, December 30, 1971 – This photograph shows Manson as a 16-year-old in Philadelphia.

CHARLES MANSON

LOS ANGELES, December 18, 1969 – Indicted with five other members of "The Family" in the Tate-LaBianca murders, Manson is brought to Los Angeles City Jail from Independence, California where he was being held after a police raid on the Family's temporary home at Spahn Movie Ranch.

LOS ANGELES, December 9, 1969 – Manson
fixed this hypnotic stare periodically throughout
his murder trial on members of the jury as
well as on the judge and Chief Prosecutor
Vincent Bugliosi.

OPPOSITE: **LOS ANGELES, December 22, 1970 –
Charles Manson, with a goatee and mustache,
appears to leer angrily as he is taken to court
for the prosecution's closing arguments.**

Lucas ordered him from the courtroom for refusing to face the jurists' bench. Manson's attorney, Irving Kanarek, tried several times to get his client to face the judge but to no avail. BOTTOM: **LOS ANGELES, March 29, 1971 –** Throughout the Tate-LaBianca murder trial, members of the Manson Family have maintained expected to return a verdict in the penalty phase of the trial, the girls showed up with completely shaved heads, in apparent imitation of Manson who shaved his head and beard last week. Clockwise from upper left: Cappy, Kathy, Mary, Sandy, and Brenda. The girls go by several aliases, often swapping names with each other.

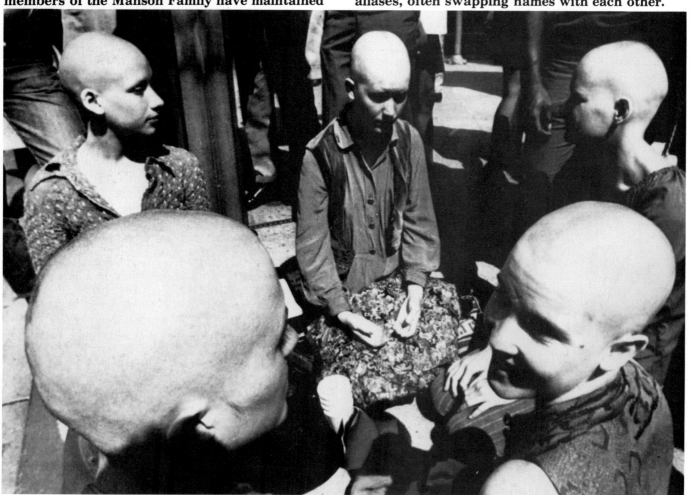

CHARLES MANSON

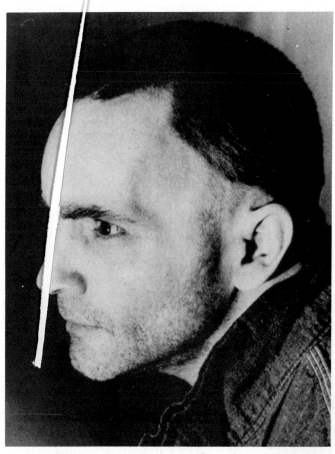

LOS ANGELES, March 11, 1971 – Three poses of Manson after he shaved his head and beard and carved a swastika symbol on his forehead.
ABOVE: March 24, 1971 – Manson scowling after a session during which Leslie Van Houten's attorney, Maxwell Keith, suggested that Manson had made the girl a "sacrificial lamb," and that she and the other two female defendants were victims of a "frightful influence that still permeates these girls' sick minds in this courtroom."
LEFT: April 19, 1971 – Manson after hearing the jury return the death sentence on him and his three female co-defendants. Defense attorneys have indicated they will make motions for a new trial and attempt to question individual jurors about possible outside influences on their verdict.

CHARLES MANSON

MCKINNEY, TEXAS February 16, 1970 – Charles "Tex" Watson, charged in California with the Tate-LaBianca murders, sits in Collin County Courtroom during a hearing on whether or not to extradite Watson to California. (His defense attorneys were later to make the most of Watson's "all-American, Joe College" looks to play down the likelihood that he could have participated so willingly in the Tate-LaBianca murders. Tried and convicted separately, Watson was given the death sentence.)

CHARLES MANSON

PREVIEW EDITION
TUESDAY
Los Angeles Times LATE SPORTS
MANSON GUILTY, NIXON DECLARES
Defense Says Mistrial Will Be Asked

LOS ANGELES, August, 1970 – A copy of the Los Angeles Times is pictured in front of the Hall of Justice here after Charles Manson held up a copy in front of the jury at his murder trial. Earlier, Judge Older refused to call a mistrial over the remarks made in Denver by President Nixon. For fear of prejudicing the jury, all newspapers have been banned from the courtroom, but Manson apparently was able to sneak the paper in and hold it up for the jury to see. To determine if a mistrial must be called, the jury members were questioned about seeing the headlines shown them. In general, those that did see it when Manson held it up indicated that they were not about to let anyone, even the President, decide this case for them. The trial continued.

CHARLES MANSON

SACRAMENTO, CALIFORNIA, September 5, 1975 – Lynette "Squeaky" Fromme of the Manson Family is led away by security guards after she drew a pistol and aimed it at at President Gerald Ford in downtown Sacramento.

OPPOSITE PAGE: LOS ANGELES, Aprl 22, 1971 – On his way to San Quentin's death row, 36-year-old Manson will be processed as the row's ninety-fourth inmate. He will be brought back to Los Angeles to stand trial in connection with the Gary Hinman–Donald "Shorty" Shea murders.

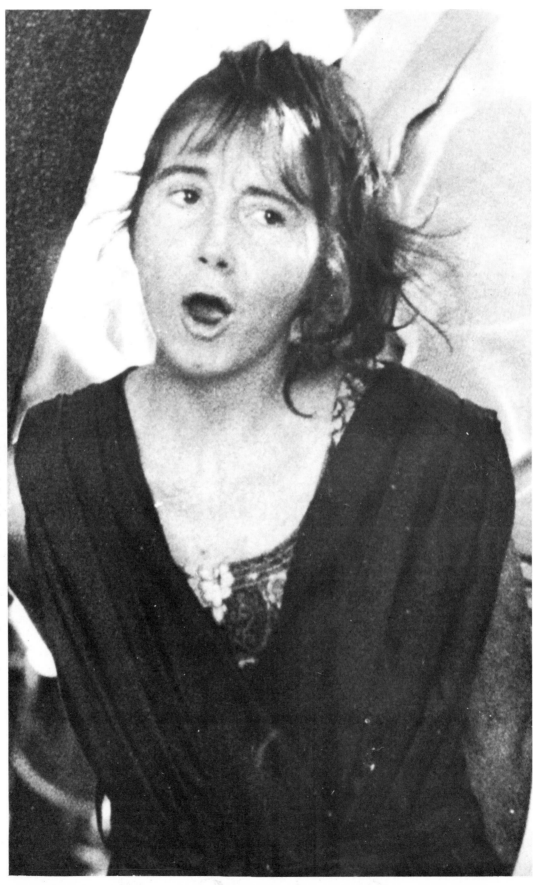

INDEX